Collins

Mission:
français

- Yo
  b
- It

pil Book 1

2 4 DEC 2012

Marie-Thérèse Bougard and Glennis Pve

Series Editor: Linz

William Collins's dream of knowledge for all began with the publication of his first book in 1819. A self-educated mill worker, he not only enriched millions of lives, but also founded a flourishing publishing house. Today, staying true to this spirit, Collins books are packed with inspiration, innovation and practical expertise. They place you at the centre of a world of possibility and give you exactly what you need to explore it.

Collins. Freedom to teach.

Published by Collins
An imprint of HarperCollins*Publishers*
77–85 Fulham Palace Road
Hammersmith
London
W6 8JB

Browse the complete Collins catalogue at
www.harpercollins.co.uk

10 9 8 7 6 5 4 3 2 1

ISBN-13 978-0-00-751341-3

The authors assert their moral rights to be identified as the authors of this work.

British Library Cataloguing in Publication Data
A catalogue record for this publication is available from the British Library.

Commissioned by Katie Sergeant
Series concept by Linzy Dickinson
Project managed by Elektra Media Ltd
Development edited by Ginny March
Copy-edited by Sarah Patey
Proofread by Leah Morin
Concept design by Elektra Media Ltd
Illustrations by Elektra Media Ltd
Typeset by Jouve India Private Limited
Cover design by Angela English

Printed and bound by L.E.G.O. S.p.A. Italy

Acknowledgements
The publishers wish to thank the following for permission to reproduce photographs. Every effort has been made to trace copyright holders and to obtain their permission for the use of copyright materials. The publishers will gladly receive any information enabling them to rectify any error or omission at the first opportunity.

Cover tl prochasson Frederic/Shutterstock, cover tr haraldmuc/Shutterstock, cover br Kirsz Marcin/Shutterstock, cover bl Roman Sigaev/Shutterstock, p 6tl FrankyDeMeyer/iStockphoto, p 6tr africa924/iStockphoto, p 6bl SlidePix/iStockphoto, p 6br Caleb Foster/Shutterstock, P 11c Photoshot/Columbia Pictures, p 11b Photoshot, p16tl CostinT/iStockphoto, p 16tc Ryan Lindsay/iStockphoto, p 16tr Rudy Mareel/Shutterstock, p 16bl Tupungato/iStockphoto, p 16bc Chris Hepburn/iStockphoto, p 16br 77photo/iStockphoto, p 18tl Jean-Yves Benedeyt/iStockphoto, p 18tcl Steve Geer/iStockphoto, p 18tcr Cristian Lazzari/iStockphoto, p 18tr Albert Barr/iStockphoto, p 18bcl Meredith Lamb/iStockphoto, p 18bcr Christophe Testi/iStockphoto, p 18br Kim Walker/Robert Harding World Imagery/Corbis, p 19 nikitsin.smugmug.com/Shutterstock p 25tl jean gill/iStockphoto, p 25tcl stockcam/iStockphoto, p 25tcr Retna/Photoshot, p25tr img85h/iStockphoto, p 25bl Helena Lovincic/iStockphoto, p 25bcl Mikhail Zahranichny/Shutterstock, p 25bcr S. Greg Panosian/iStockphoto, p 25br vvoe/Shutterstock, p 30t tupungato/iStockphoto, p 30bl Sapsiwai/Shutterstock, p 30br aiok/Shutterstock, p 54t gorillaimages/Shutterstock, p 54cl photofriday/Shutterstock, p 54cr Thierry Maffeis/Shutterstock, p 54bl MilousSK/Shutterstock, p 54br Elena Blokhina/Shutterstock, p 63 *Rendez vous place Stanislas* Régine Datin/Nancy Tourisme, p 78cl *VolcanBul* Camus-Vulcania, p 78cr Puy du Fou, p 78bl glen gaffney/Shutterstock, p 78br Barbara Boensch/image/imagebroker.net/Superstock, p 79l Biscaro/Masterfile/VISUALPHOTOS.COM, p 79cl Prisma/Superstock, p 79cr COLIN Matthieu/hemi/Hemis.fr/SuperStock, p 79r imagebroker.net/SuperStock, p 81cl Thomas Pozzo di Borgo/iStockphoto, p81cr Valery Bareta/iStockphoto, p81r Ann Taylor-Hughes/iStockphoto, p 82 *cone* Luc Olivier 2010, p 85 Les Editions Albert René/Goscinny-Uderzo/S.Cambon, p 89 Ana Abejon/iStockphoto, p 94 ACI (JL AUDY-F JUILLE)/Kuka/BCBG/FUTUROSCOPE, p 95 Futuroscope_Creation/Fotolia/Studio Ludo/S LAVAL/Robothespian – © Engineered Arts Limited 2012 – D LAMING, Architecte – M Vimenet – Toutain – Chorégraphies: Mourad Merzouki – CCN Créteil et du Val-de-Marne/Compagnie Käfig, p 102t cesc_assawin/Shutterstock, p 102cl *Mona Lisa*, c.1503-6 (oil on panel), Vinci, Leonardo da (1452-1519)/Louvre, Paris, France/Giraudon/The Bridgeman Art Library, p 102cr OlegAlbinsky/Shutterstock, p 102bl pisaphotography/Shutterstock, p 102br Nightman1965/Shutterstock, p 108l *The Little Dancer* (Petite danseuse de quatorze ans) 1921 (polychrome bronze, satin ribbon & wood), Degas, Edgar (1834–1917)/Private Collection/Photo Christie's Images/The Bridgeman Art Library, p 108r *Little Dancer*, Aged 14, viewed from the back (polychrome bronze, satin ribbon & wood), Degas, Edgar (1834–1917)/Private Collection/Photo Christie's Images/The Bridgeman Art Library, p 109t *The Siesta*, 1891–2 (oil on canvas), Gauguin, Paul (1848–1903)/Private Collection/Peter Willi/The Bridgeman Art Library, p 109c *Le Quai St. Michel and Notre Dame*, 1901 (oil on canvas), Luce, Maximilien (1858–1941)/Musee d'Orsay, Paris, France/Gift of Mr and Mrs Henry H. Timken/The Bridgeman Art Library, p110l Roberto Esposti/Alamy, p 110c 2013 LES EDITIONS ALBERT RENE/GOSCINNY-UDERZO, p 100r Hergé/Moulinsart 2013, p 111 *Titeuf*, Tome 9 by Zep/2002 – EDITIONS GLENAT, p 112 Jorge Felix Costa/Shutterstock, p 113l CDA/Guillemot/akg-images, p 113cl xc/Shutterstock, p 113cr sam100/Shutterstock, p 113r pisaphotography/Shutterstock, p 114l Christian Bertrand/Shutterstock, p114r Michel Bouvet, p 115l AFP/Getty Images, p 115cl forestpath/Shutterstock, p 115cr Nadiia Gerbish/Shutterstock, p 115r AFP/Getty Images, p 119 *Young Girls at the Piano*, 1892 (gouache), Renoir, Pierre-Auguste (1841–1919)/Private Collection/The Bridgeman Art Library, p 124t xc/Shutterstock, p 124b C Jones/Shutterstock, p125t Sean Nel/Shutterstock, p 125b Jack.Q/Shutterstock.

Tableau des contenus

Le monde francophone

- La France
- L'Europe
- Capitale: Paris
- Population: 65 635 000

- Le Sénégal
- L'Afrique
- Capitale: Dakar
- Population: 12 855 153

- Le Canada
- L'Amérique du nord
- Capitale: Ottawa
- Population: 35 002 447

- La Martinique
- L'Amérique du nord
- Capitale: Fort de France
- Population: 394 173

Découverte du monde:

The French-speaking world – *le monde francophone* – is made up of many countries in different parts of the world. These countries have lots in common apart from the French language, but they are also different in many ways. If you visited all the French-speaking countries of the world you'd see a whole range of landscapes. You'd experience many different ways of life as well as many rich cultures and traditions. As you learn the French language, you'll discover some of these places and all that they have to offer.

Le savais-tu?

More than two hundred million people speak French.

French is spoken on five continents.

Sixty per cent of French speakers are under the age of 30.

Every year, on 20 March, people all around the world celebrate *la Journée internationale de la francophonie* (International Francophone Day).

 1

Parle à quatre personnes dans ta classe.
Speak to four people in your class.

Exemple
A Salut! Comment tu t'appelles?
B Je m'appelle _____. Et toi, comment tu t'appelles?

 2

Associe les mots anglais et les mots français pour les continents.
Match the English and French words for the continents.

l'Europe — Europe
l'Asie — Asia
l'Amérique du nord — South America
l'Amérique du sud — Australia
l'Antarctique — Africa
l'Australie — North America
l'Afrique — Antarctica

3

À deux, faites une liste de pays francophones.
In pairs, make a list of French-speaking countries.

Module 1: Ta mission...

- Say how I feel and ask other people
- Describe myself and other people
- Make negative sentences
- Use adjectives correctly
- Talk about my family

- Say how old I am and how old other people are
- Talk about countries, nationalities and languages
- Use the correct form of a regular –er verb
- Talk about the place I live in
- Use *un*, *une* and *des*

Objectifs
- Say how I feel and ask other people
- Use the correct spelling of some adjectives

Langue et grammaire

Asking someone how they are
Here are three ways of asking this question:

Ça va?	To use with a friend or someone you know very well
Comment ça va?	To use with a young person you don't know well
Comment allez-vous?	To use with an adult who isn't a close friend

Using verbs (doing words)
Learning to use French verbs is very important. Regular verbs follow patterns you can learn to use (see page 130). Those that don't follow these patterns are called irregular verbs.

To talk about how you are feeling you can use the verb être (to be). It's an irregular verb.

Look at how it works:

je suis	I am	*tu es*	you are
il est	he is	*elle est*	she is

Using adjectives (describing words)
In French, the spelling of an adjective often changes depending on the person or thing it is describing. For example, many have an extra 'e' at the end to show that they are describing a girl or woman.

Pronunciation
The cedilla mark under the letter 'c' (ç) before the letters 'a', 'o' and 'u' makes it sound like the letter 's'. The letter 'c' always sounds like the letter 's' in front of the letters 'e' and 'i'.

Listen to the sound of the letter é, for example in the word *fatigué*.

---

① Écoute, écris la bonne lettre (a–f) et dessine le bon symbole.

Listen, write the correct letter and draw the correct symbol.

Exemple 1f 😕

a Ça va bien, merci. Et vous?	b Ça va super bien.
c Ça va très mal aujourd'hui.	d Bof! Pas mal.
e Mmm, comme ci comme ça.	f Ça va mal.

② Écoute et choisis la bonne image (A–F) pour chaque personne.

Listen and choose the correct picture for each person.

Justine __C__   Sophie ____   Félix ____

Maeva ____   Madame Leroy ____   Lucas ____

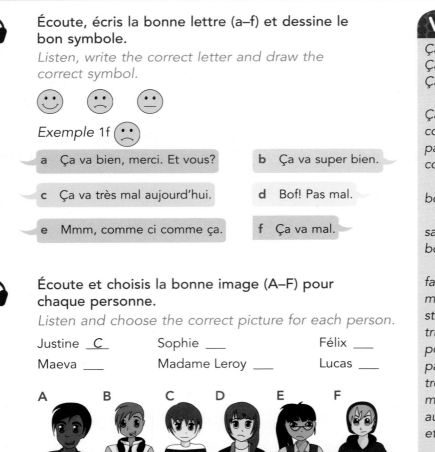

A   B   C   D   E   F

Vocabulaire

Ça va?	How are you?
Ça va.	I'm well.
Ça va (super) bien.	I'm (really) well.
Ça va mal.	I'm not very well.
comment	how, what
pas mal	not bad, okay
comme ci comme ça	so-so
bof!	something to say if you're not bothered
salut	hi
bonjour	hello, good morning
fatigué(e)	tired
malade	ill
stressé(e)	stressed-out
triste	sad
pourquoi?	why?
parce que	because
très	very
merci	thank you, thanks
aujourd'hui	today
et toi? / et vous?	and you?
ah bon?	oh really?

3 Fais un sondage. Parle à 10 personnes. Écris un nom et coche le bon symbole pour chaque personne.

Do a survey. Speak to 10 people. Write a name and tick the correct symbol for each person.

Before you speak, listen again to the recording and notice how the speakers raise their voice when they ask a question. This is the easiest way to ask a question. Practise this with the question words in the vocabulary list and then try to do the same when you do your survey.

Exemple

A Salut Sophie!

B Salut.

A Ça va?

B Ça va bien. Et toi?

Nom	☺	☹	😐
Sophie	✓		

Voie express

Have you studied some of this language before? Do you know how to ask how someone is? That's great. Check with your teacher which exercises you should do. Then you may be able to move on to some more challenging ones. Make sure you learn all the words in the vocabulary list thoroughly and that you can use the verb *être* correctly to say how you are and how someone else is.

4 Lis les conversations et trouve la différence dans **la dernière ligne**. Explique la différence à ton partenaire.

Read the conversations and find the difference in the last line. Explain the difference to your partner.

Lucas	Salut Justine. Ça va?		**Maeva**	Salut Abdou. Ça va?
Justine	Ca va merci, Lucas! Et toi?		**Abdou**	Ça va merci, Maeva! Et toi?
Lucas	Ça va mal.		**Maeva**	Ça va mal.
Justine	Ah bon, pourquoi?		**Abdou**	Ah bon, pourquoi?
Lucas	Parce que je suis fatigué.		**Maeva**	Parce que je suis fatiguée.

5 Regarde les images et écris des conversations comme celles de l'exercice 4. Attention aux adjectifs! ⭐

Look at the pictures and write conversations like those in exercise 4. Be careful with the adjectives!

6 À deux, choisissez un de vos dialogues et lisez-le à haute voix.

In pairs, choose one of your dialogues and read it out loud.

Objectifs
- Describe myself and other people
- Make negative sentences

Langue et grammaire

Using the verb *être*
You learned how to say 'I am' using the verb *être* in the previous topic. Here is a reminder of the other forms of the same verb that you looked at:

je suis	I am	*tu es*	you are
il est	he is	*elle est*	she is

Making a negative sentence
Use *ne* and *pas* around a verb to make it negative. For example:

Je suis timide.	I'm shy.
*Je **ne** suis **pas** timide.*	I'm not shy.
Il est drôle.	He's funny.
*Il **n'**est **pas** drôle.*	He isn't funny.
Elle est sympa.	She's friendly.
*Elle **n'**est **pas** sympa.*	She isn't friendly.

Notice how 'ne' changes to 'n' when the verb starts with a vowel.

Asking what someone is like
Ask:

Tu es comment?	What are you like?
Il/Elle est comment?	What is he/she like?

Remember, your voice must go up to sound like a question.

Pronunciation
If a word in French ends in a 't', 's' or 'd', you don't pronounce the last letter. For example:
bavard, intelligent
If a word ends in 'te' or 'de' then you do pronounce the 't' or 'd'. For example, *intelligen**te**, bavar**de**.*

Écoute et lis. Vrai ou faux?
Listen and read. True or false?

1 Manon est sympa.
2 Félix est drôle.
3 Justine est intelligente.
4 Maeva est bavarde.
5 Abdou est timide.
6 Nicolas est raisonnable.
7 Lucas est intelligent et paresseux.
8 Sophie est impatiente.

Écoute encore et corrige les erreurs de l'exercice 1. Choisis les adjectifs dans la liste.
Listen again and correct the mistakes in exercise 1. Choose the adjectives from the list.

raisonnable	bavard(e)	intelligent(e)	impatient(e)

Justine est *bavarde*.   Nicolas est _____.
Maeva est _____.   Sophie est _____.

Vocabulaire

sympa	friendly, nice
drôle	funny
intelligent(e)	intelligent
raisonnable	sensible
impatient(e)	impatient
timide	shy
bavard(e)	chatty
paresseux(–euse)	lazy
Je pense que...	I think that...
C'est vrai.	It's true.
C'est faux.	It's false/ wrong.
à mon avis	in my opinion
pas du tout	not at all
un peu	a little, a bit
assez	quite
trop	too much
mais	but
aussi	also
et	and

3 À deux, faites un jeu de mémoire.
In pairs, play a memory game.

Exemple
A Justine est comment?
B À mon avis, Justine est sympa.
A Non, c'est faux. Elle est bavarde.

Voie express

You need to be able to use adjectives correctly and describe what someone is not like as well as what they are like. When you learn the words in the vocabulary list, also learn which ones change their endings. Using the words in exercise 4 is a good way to improve a piece of writing, so make sure you include some of these in your work.

4 Résous les anagrammes et écris les mots dans l'ordre des mots anglais.
Solve the anagrams and write the words in the order that they are shown in English.

èrst	epunu	prot	sezas	uspottuda
not at all	a little	quite	very	too

5 Lis le texte. Associe les phrases soulignées avec les phrases en anglais.
Read the text. Match the underlined phrases with the phrases in English.

a very intelligent   *très intelligente*

b in my opinion   _____

c too impatient   _____

d quite intelligent too   _____

e I think that   _____

f not at all shy   _____

g but   _____

Salut! Je m'appelle Gwen. <u>Je pense que</u> je suis <u>très intelligente</u> et raisonnable. Je ne suis <u>pas du tout timide.</u>
Voici Peter! <u>À mon avis</u> il est sympa et <u>assez intelligent aussi</u>, <u>mais</u> il est <u>trop impatient.</u>

6 Écris un autre paragraphe sur toi et un de tes amis. ⭐
Write another paragraph about yourself and one of your friends.

7 Parlez à deux. Décrivez ces personnages.
Work in pairs. Describe these characters.

A Il/elle est comment?
B À mon avis il/elle est _____,
   il/elle n'est pas _____.
A Je pense qu'il/elle s'appelle _____.
B Oui, c'est vrai. / Non c'est faux.

Objectifs
- Describe myself and other people
- Use adjectives correctly

Langue et grammaire

Describing people

To describe someone's height and build, use the verb *être*. You have seen this in the last two topics:

je suis petit	I am small
je ne suis pas grand	I am not tall

Use the verb *avoir* to talk about the kind of hair and eyes someone has. Look at how this verb works:

j'ai	I have
tu as	you have
il a	he has
elle a	she has

Using adjectives correctly

You've already seen how an adjective can change depending on whether it is describing a male or female person. An adjective also changes if it is describing more than one thing or more than one person. For example, the words for eyes and hair are both plural so you add an 's' to adjectives you use to describe them:

les yeux bleus	blue eyes
les cheveux blonds	blond hair

The adjective *marron* is unusual and does **not** change:

les yeux marron	brown eyes

Adjectives usually go after the noun they are describing. Look at the examples above again.

Pronunciation

The letter 'x' at the end of a word is silent: *cheveux, yeux*

The letter combination *aille* is pronounced like the English word 'eye': *de taille moyenne*.

a Regarde les adjectifs et écris les bonnes initiales. (BB, DD, RR, II, PP)

Look at the adjectives and write the correct initials by each.

1 gros *PP*   2 grande

3 petit   4 petite

5 grand   6 de taille moyenne

7 mince

b Écoute et écris les bonnes initiales. (1–7)

Listen and write the correct initials.

2 Lis et écris le bon numéro pour chaque personnage.

Read and write the correct number for each character.

Je dessine. J'invente des personnages amusants. Regarde!

Bernard Bavard

Daphné Drôle

Ronald Raisonnable

Irène Intelligente

Pierre Paresseux

BB ___   DD ___   RR ___   II ___   PP ___

1 | Je ne suis pas petite et je ne suis pas grosse.

2 | Je ne suis pas grosse mais je suis petite.

3 | Je suis grand et je ne suis pas gros.

4 | Je ne suis pas grand, mais je suis gros.

5 | Je ne suis pas grand, je ne suis pas petit.

3 Jouez à deux. Décrivez un personnage. C'est qui?
Play in pairs. Describe a character. Who is it?

Exemple

A Elle est petite et elle est de taille moyenne.

B Je pense que c'est _____.

A Oui, c'est ça. / Non, c'est faux.

4 **a** Regarde encore les personnages. Écoute, écris les bonnes initiales et choisis les bons cheveux. (1–5)
Look again at the characters. Listen, write the correct initials and choose the correct description of their hair.

   a   les cheveux courts et blonds

   b   les cheveux mi-longs et noirs

   c   les cheveux longs et bruns

   d   les cheveux longs et noirs

   e   les cheveux courts et bruns

Exemple   **1** DD c

b Écoute encore et choisis la bonne description des yeux.
Listen again and choose the correct description of their eyes.

| les yeux gris | les yeux bleus | les yeux marron | les yeux verts |

Vocabulaire	
grand(e)	tall/big
petit(e)	short/small
de taille moyenne	medium height
mince	thin
gros(se)	fat
les cheveux blonds/ bruns/noirs/roux	blond/brown/ black/red hair
les cheveux longs/ courts/mi-longs	long/short/ medium-length hair
les yeux bleus/ verts/marron/gris	blue/green/ brown/grey eyes
qui	who
un personnage	a cartoon character
Oui, c'est ça.	Yes, that's right.
Non, c'est faux.	No, that's wrong.

5 Réécris les textes avec les bonnes informations. ⭐
Rewrite the text with the correct information.

a Salut! Je m'appelle Pierre Paresseux. Je suis grand et mince. J'ai les cheveux courts et roux et j'ai les yeux bleus.

b Salut! Je m'appelle Bernard Bavard. Je suis petit et gros. J'ai les cheveux longs et noirs et j'ai les yeux marron.

c Bonjour! Je m'appelle Irène Intelligente. Je suis très petite et grosse. J'ai les cheveux courts et bruns et j'ai les yeux gris.

d Bonjour! Je m'appelle Daphné Drôle. Je suis grande et j'ai les cheveux courts et blonds.

e Salut! Je m'appelle Ronald Raisonnable. Je suis très grand et j'ai les cheveux courts et noirs.

Voie express
The important thing in this topic is that you learn how to describe what someone looks like using the verbs *être* and *avoir*. Also make sure that you know how to change an adjective depending on who or what it describes.

Exemple

a Salut! Je m'appelle Pierre Paresseux. Je suis petit et gros. J'ai les cheveux courts et les yeux verts.

Objectifs
- Talk about my family
- Say how old I am and how old other people are

Langue et grammaire

Using masculine and feminine nouns

Nouns in French are masculine or feminine. Use *un* to mean 'a' for a masculine noun and *une* to mean 'a' for a feminine noun:

un frère   a brother   *une sœur*   a sister

Making a noun plural

In most cases, add 's' just like in English:

J'ai deux frères.   I have two brothers.
J'ai trois sœurs.   I have three sisters.

Talking about age

Use the verb *avoir* to talk about age. You learned how to use *avoir* in the previous topic.

J'ai douze ans.   I'm twelve years old.
Tu as quel âge?   How old are you?
Il/elle a seize ans.   He/she is sixteen years old.

Using 'my' and your'

There are three French words for 'my' and three for 'your'. To know which word to use, check whether the noun that comes after it is masculine, feminine or plural.

	masculine	feminine	plural
my	*mon*	*ma*	*mes*
your	*ton*	*ta*	*tes*

For example:

mon frère   my brother   *ton frère*   your brother
ma sœur   my sister   *ta sœur*   your sister
mes frères my brothers   *tes sœurs*   your sisters

Pronunciation

If a word ending in 's' or 'x' is followed by a word beginning with a vowel, you pronounce the 's' or 'x', although usually it is silent. For example: *trois ans*

1 a Quels sont les numéros dans l'image? Écris le français et l'anglais.

What are the numbers in the wordsnake? Write the French and the English.

neufseptuntroisdixhuitquatredeuxcinqsix

b Écoute et vérifie tes réponses.

Listen and check your answers.

2 Lis et écoute. Qui dit les phrases – Justine, Lucas ou Manon?

Read and listen. Who says these sentences – Justine, Lucas or Manon?

1 Tu as une grande famille?   *Justine*

2 J'ai une petite famille.

3 J'ai une sœur.

4 J'ai deux sœurs.

5 Je n'ai pas de sœur.

6 Je n'ai pas de frère.

7 J'ai un frère.

8 Je suis fille unique.

9 J'ai une grande famille.

Vocabulaire

une famille	a family
une sœur	a sister
un frère	a brother
fils unique	only child (boy)
fille unique	only child (girl)
un enfant	a child
Tu as quel âge?	How old are you?
Il/elle a quel âge?	How old is he/she?

3 Regarde les traductions anglaises. Complète les phrases françaises avec les mots dans la boîte.

Look at the English translations. Complete the French sentences with the words from the box.

> frère   n'ai   petite   suis   deux

1 J'ai une _____ famille.   I have a small family.

2 J'ai un _____.   I have one brother.

3 Je _____ pas de frère.   I don't have any brothers.

4 Je _____ fille unique.   I'm an only child.

4 Lis les phrases de l'exercise 2. Regarde le camembert. Qui a la famille type?

Read the sentences in exercise 2. Look at the pie chart. Who has the most common type of family?

5 Quelle est la famille type pour ta classe? Fais un sondage et crée une infographie.

What is the most common type of family in your class? Do a survey and create a pie chart.

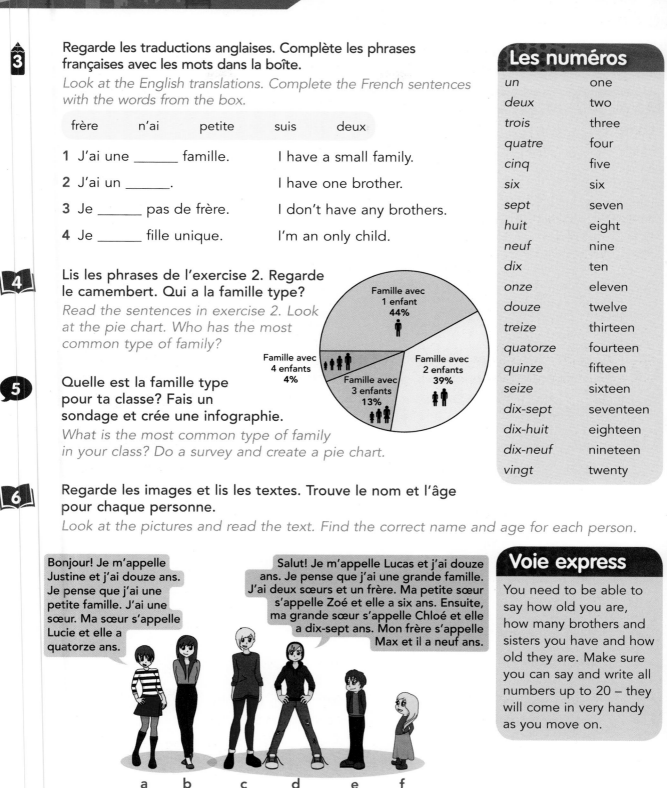

Les numéros

un	one
deux	two
trois	three
quatre	four
cinq	five
six	six
sept	seven
huit	eight
neuf	nine
dix	ten
onze	eleven
douze	twelve
treize	thirteen
quatorze	fourteen
quinze	fifteen
seize	sixteen
dix-sept	seventeen
dix-huit	eighteen
dix-neuf	nineteen
vingt	twenty

Famille avec 1 enfant 44%

Famille avec 4 enfants 4%

Famille avec 3 enfants 13%

Famille avec 2 enfants 39%

6 Regarde les images et lis les textes. Trouve le nom et l'âge pour chaque personne.

Look at the pictures and read the text. Find the correct name and age for each person.

Bonjour! Je m'appelle Justine et j'ai douze ans. Je pense que j'ai une petite famille. J'ai une sœur. Ma sœur s'appelle Lucie et elle a quatorze ans.

Salut! Je m'appelle Lucas et j'ai douze ans. Je pense que j'ai une grande famille. J'ai deux sœurs et un frère. Ma petite sœur s'appelle Zoé et elle a six ans. Ensuite, ma grande sœur s'appelle Chloé et elle a dix-sept ans. Mon frère s'appelle Max et il a neuf ans.

Voie express

You need to be able to say how old you are, how many brothers and sisters you have and how old they are. Make sure you can say and write all numbers up to 20 – they will come in very handy as you move on.

a   b   c   d   e   f

7 Relis les textes de l'exercice 6 et décris ta famille.

Read the texts in exercise 6 again and write about your family.

Objectifs
- Talk about countries, nationalities and languages
- Use the correct form of a regular –er verb

Langue et grammaire

Using verbs

Verbs are used to talk about what people do. In French, the most common type of verbs are –er verbs, like *habiter* (to live) and *parler* (to speak):

parler	to speak	habiter	to live
je parle	I speak	j'habite	I live
tu parles	you speak	tu habites	you live
il/elle parle	he/she speaks	il/elle habite	he/she lives

Notice how *je* changes in *j'habite*. You've seen this before with *j'ai* (I have). This is because the letter 'h' in French is silent.

Using nouns

All nouns in French are either masculine or feminine, not just the ones to do with people. Remember to use *le* (the) or *un* (a/an) with a masculine noun and *la* (the) or *une* (a/an) with a feminine noun.

Questions

The French word *où* means 'where'. If you write *ou* without the accent, it sounds the same but it means 'or', so make sure you remember the accent!

To ask someone where they live:
Tu habites où?

Écoute. Associe les villes (a–f) et les pays (1–6).
Listen. Match the towns (a–f) with the countries (1–6).

a Montréal   **c** Dakar   **e** Saint-Pierre

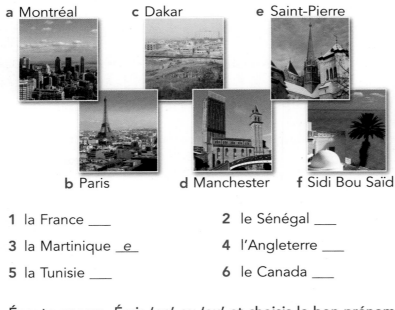

b Paris   **d** Manchester   **f** Sidi Bou Saïd

1 la France ___   **2** le Sénégal ___

3 la Martinique _e_   **4** l'Angleterre ___

5 la Tunisie ___   **6** le Canada ___

Vocabulaire

la France	France
l'Angleterre (f)	England
la Tunisie	Tunisia
la Martinique	Martinique
le Canada	Canada
le Sénégal	Senegal
français(e)	French
anglais(e)	English
tunisien(ne)	Tunisian
martiniquais(e)	from Martinique
canadien(ne)	Canadian
sénégalais(e)	Senegalese
le français	French (lang.)
l'anglais (m)	English (lang.)
l'arabe (m)	Arabic (lang.)
le créole	Creole (lang.)
un père	father
une mère	mother
le pays	country
la ville	town
où	where
parler	to speak

Écoute encore. Écris 'en' ou 'au' et choisis le bon prénom.
Listen again. Fill the gaps with en *or* au *and choose the correct name.*

Manon   Marc   Emma   Hugo   Marie   Amal

1 J'habite ___ Martinique.   **2** J'habite ___ France.   **3** J'habite ___ Sénégal.

4 J'habite ___ Angleterre.   **5** J'habite ___ Canada.   **6** J'habite ___ Tunisie.

3 Regarde les informations des exercices 1 et 2. Parlez à deux.

Look at the information in exercises 1 and 2. Speak in pairs.

Exemple

A Salut! Tu t'appelles comment?

B Je m'appelle Emma.

A Tu habites où, Emma?

B J'habite en/au _____ , à _____ .

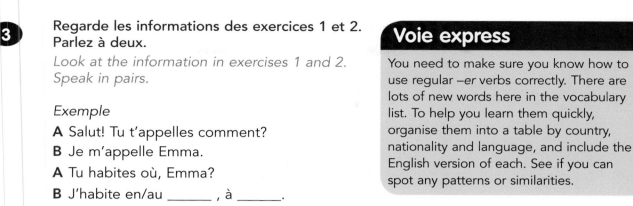

Voie express

You need to make sure you know how to use regular –*er* verbs correctly. There are lots of new words here in the vocabulary list. To help you learn them quickly, organise them into a table by country, nationality and language, and include the English version of each. See if you can spot any patterns or similarities.

4 Écris d'autres conversations, par exemple sur d'autres pays francophones.

Write other versions of the conversation, for example about other Francophone countries.

5 Lis le 'Forum des francophones' et réponds aux questions en anglais.

Read the 'Forum des francophones' and answer the questions in English.

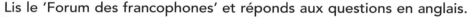

Le Forum des Francopho... ✕

http://leforumdesfrancophones.fr/index.php?showtopic=1746

Le forum des francophones

blog   membres   aider   rechercher   calendrier

▶ **Le forum des francophones > Introductions** | répondre | sujet | vote |

▶ **Bonjour**

	le 29 mars, 12h05
Emma	J'habite à Saint-Pierre en Martinique. Je suis martiniquaise et je parle français, mais je parle créole aussi. À bientôt, Emma

	le 29 mars, 14h32
Amal	J'habite à Sidi Bou Saïd en Tunisie. Je suis tunisienne et je parle français, mais je parle arabe aussi. Salut, Amal

	le 29 mars, 16h04
Marc	J'habite à Manchester en Angleterre. Je suis anglais et je parle anglais et français parce que mon père est anglais mais ma mère est française. À bientôt, Marc

1 What country does Emma live in?

2 How many languages does Emma speak?

3 What nationality is Amal?

4 Which two languages does Amal speak?

5 What nationality is Marc's mum?

6 Does Marc speak French?

6 Écris au 'Forum des francophones'.

Write about yourself on the 'Forum des francophones'.

Objectifs:
- Talk about the place I live in
- Use *un, une, des*

Langue et grammaire

Il y a

You can use the phrase *il y a* to talk about what there is in a place. This phrase can mean both 'there is' and 'there are' so it is very useful. For example: *Qu'est-ce qu'il y a à Paris? Il y a des monuments. Il n'y a pas de volcan!*

What is there in Paris? There are monuments. There is no volcano!

Notice that *il n'y a pas* is always followed by *de*, instead of *un, une* or *des*.

Using nouns

You've already seen how to use *un* and *une* when talking about one item. To talk about more than one item, use *des*, which means 'some'.
Look at these examples:

un magasin	a shop
des magasins	some shops
une plage	a beach
des plages	some beaches

Mon Blog

Un portrait de ma ville: Saint Pierre – mes photos.

a b c d

e f g h

Qui suis-je?

Salut tout le monde! Je m'appelle Emma. J'ai 12 ans et j'habite à Saint Pierre, en Martinique.

Accueil
Mes copains
Ma famille
Album photos

Vocabulaire

un village	a village
une plage	a beach
un volcan	a volcano
des ruines	ruins
un marché	a market
une bibliothèque	a library
une gare	a station
une ferme	a farm
un magasin	a shop
un stade	a stadium
un cinéma	a cinema
un centre commercial	a shopping centre
un port	a port
une église	a church
une patinoire	an ice-rink
une tante	an aunt
un oncle	an uncle
un musée	a museum
dans	in

1 Trouve le bon mot pour chaque photo de Saint-Pierre. Écris 'un', 'une' ou 'des'.

Find the correct word for each photo of Saint-Pierre. Write un, une or des.

plageportmagasinsmuséeégliseruinesmarchévolcan

Exemple

a un port

2 Écoute et note l'ordre des photos.

Listen and note down the order of the photos.

a ___   b ___   c ___   d ___   e ___   f ___   g _1_   h ___

3 Écoute Hugo. Qu'est-ce qu'il y a à Montréal? Qu'est-ce qu'il n'y a pas? Écris en anglais.
Listen to Hugo. What is there in Montreal? What isn't there? Write in English.

4 Parlez à deux.
Speak in pairs.

Exemple

A Qu'est-ce qu'il y a dans ta ville?

B Il y a ____, et il y a aussi ____, mais il n'y a pas de ____.

A Tu habites à ____?

B Oui/Non, j'habite à ____.

Petiteville

Grandeville

Superville

Extraville

5 Lis les textes et les phrases 1–10. Vrai ou faux?
Read the texts and sentences 1–10. True or false?

1 Emma's aunt lives in Fort-de-France. *Vrai*

2 Saint-Pierre is the capital of Martinique.

3 There is a library and a cinema in Fort-de-France.

4 There is no shopping centre in Fort-de-France.

5 There are trains in Martinique.

6 Hugo's uncle lives in a small village.

7 There are lots of shops in Maskinongé.

8 There isn't a farm in Maskinongé.

9 There isn't an ice-rink or a swimming pool in Maskinongé.

10 There is a stadium in Maskinongé.

Emma

J'habite à Saint-Pierre. Saint-Pierre est une petite ville, mais ma tante habite à Fort-de-France, la capitale de la Martinique. À Fort-de-France il y a une bibliothèque, il y a un cinéma et il y a un centre commercial. Mais il n'y a pas de gare parce que, ici, en Martinique, il n'y a pas de train!

J'habite à Montréal. Montréal est une très grande ville, mais mon oncle habite à Maskinongé, un petit village canadien. À Maskinongé il y a un magasin et il y a une ferme, mais il n'y a pas de patinoire, il n'y a pas de piscine et il n'y a pas de stade.

Hugo

6 Corrige les phrases fausses de l'exercice 5. Écris en français. ⭐
Correct the false sentences in exercise 5. Write in French.

Exemple

2 Fort-de-France est la capitale de la Martinique.

7 Écris un portrait de ta ville ou écris une liste.
Write a description of your town, or make a list of what there is in your town.

Voie express

If your teacher agrees, go straight to exercise 7 and create a portrait of your own town for your blog. You may need to use a dictionary to find out and learn the words for things that are in your town that are not covered in this topic. The most important thing is that you learn whether things are masculine or feminine and that you use *un*, *une* and *des* correctly.

Langue et grammaire

Asking questions

The word *comment* means 'how'. You can use it to ask how someone is or what they are like:

Comment ça va?	How are you?
Tu es comment?	What are you like?

The word *où* means 'where'. Use it to ask someone where they live:

Tu habites où?	Where do you live?

Using the verb *être* to describe people

The verb 'to be' is *être* in French:

je suis	I am	*tu es*	you are
il est	he is	*elle est*	she is

You can use it to describe height and build:

je suis petit	I am small

Using the verb *avoir* to describe people

The verb 'to have' is *avoir* in French:

j'ai	I have	*tu as*	you have
il a	he has	*elle a*	she has

You can use it to describe age or the kind of hair and eyes someone has:

J'ai douze ans.	I'm twelve years old.
Elle a les yeux bleus.	She has blue eyes.

Il y a

Use *il y a* to describe what there is in a place:

Il y a des monuments.	There are monuments.

Using regular *–er* verbs

In French, the most common type of verbs are *–er* verbs, like *habiter* (to live). This is how they work:

habiter	to live
j'habite	I live
tu habites	you live
il/elle habite	he/she lives

Making a negative sentence

Use *ne* and *pas* around a verb to make it negative. For example:

Je ne suis pas timide.	I'm not shy.

Using nouns

All nouns in French are either masculine or feminine. Use *le* (the) or *un* (a/an) with a masculine noun and *la* (the) or *une* (a/an) with a feminine noun:

le marché	a market
la ville	a town/city

To talk about more than one item, use *des*, which means 'some' or *les*:

des magasins	some shops

Using 'my' and your'

There are three French words for 'my' and three for 'your'. To know which word to use, check whether the noun that comes after it is masculine, feminine or plural.

	masculine	feminine	plural
a/an/some	*un*	*une*	*des*
the	*le*	*la*	*les*
my	*mon*	*ma*	*mes*
your	*ton*	*ta*	*tes*

Making a noun plural

In most cases, add 's' just like in English:

J'ai deux frères.	I have two brothers.

Using adjectives

Many adjectives have an extra 'e' at the end if they are describing a girl or woman:

Il est fatigué.	He is tired.
Elle est fatiguée.	She is tired.

Adjectives usually also change if they are describing plural nouns:

les yeux bleus	blue eyes

Some adjectives are irregular and do not change:

les yeux marron	brown eyes

Notice that adjectives usually go after the noun they are describing.

Vocabulaire

Les salutations

Ça va?

Ça va (super) bien.

Ça va mal.

pas mal

comme ci
  comme ça

salut

bonjour

Mots utiles

Je pense que…

à mon avis

pas du tout

très

merci

aujourd'hui

où

trop

mais

aussi

et

qui

un peu

assez

ah bon

bof!

et toi

pourquoi

parce que

comment

Les descriptions

le personnage…

stressé(e)

malade

fatigué(e)

sympa

drôle

intelligent(e)

raisonnable

impatient(e)

timide

bavard(e)

paresseux(–euse)

triste

grand(e)

petit(e)

de taille moyenne

mince

gros(se)

les cheveux…

blonds/bruns/
  noirs/roux/
  (mi-)longs/courts

les yeux…

bleus/verts/
  marron/gris

La famille

le père

la mère

la famille

la sœur

le frère

le fils unique

la fille unique

l'enfant (m)

la tante

l'oncle (m)

**Pays et
nationalités**

la France

l'Angleterre (f)

la Tunisie

la Martinique

le Canada

le Sénégal

français(e)

anglais(e)

tunisien(ne)

martiniquais(e)

canadien(ne)

sénégalais(e)

le français

l'anglais (m)

l'arabe (m)

le créole

**Questions et
réponses**

Tu as quel âge?

Il/elle a quel âge?

C'est vrai.

C'est faux.

Oui, c'est ça.

Non, c'est faux.

Numéros

un(e)

deux

trois

quatre

cinq

six

sept

huit

neuf

dix

onze

douze

treize

quatorze

quinze

seize

dix-sept

dix-huit

dix-neuf

vingt

Les endroits

le marché

la bibliothèque

la gare

la ferme

le magasin

le stade

le cinéma

le centre
commercial

le port

la plage

le volcan

les ruines

l'église (f)

le musée

la patinoire

le village

la ville

le pays

Mission accomplie?

I can…

☐ Say how I feel and ask other people

☐ Describe myself and other people

☐ Make negative sentences

☐ Use adjectives correctly

☐ Talk about my family

☐ Say how old I am and how old other people are

☐ Talk about countries, nationalities and languages

☐ Use the correct form of a regular –er verb

☐ Talk about the place I live in

☐ Use un, une and des

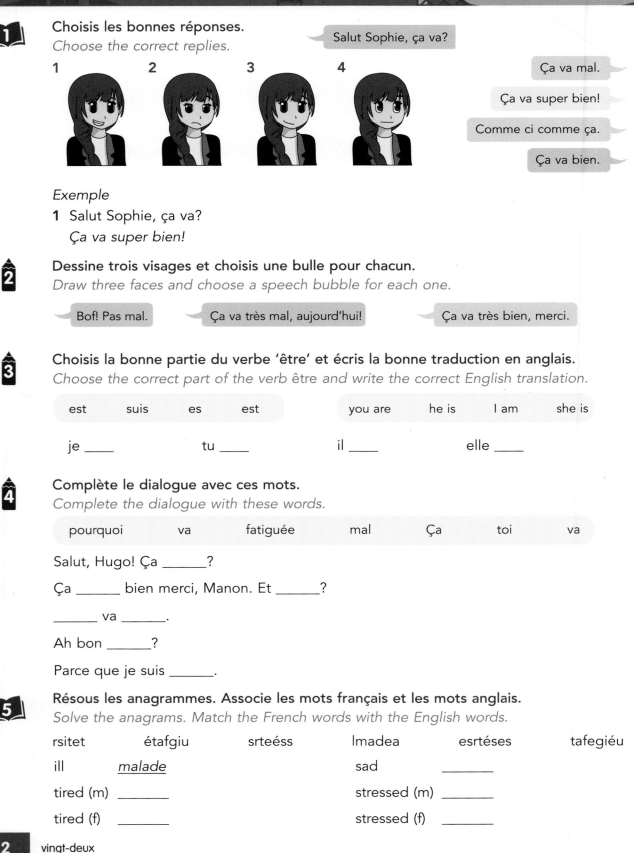

1 Choisis les bonnes réponses.
Choose the correct replies.

Salut Sophie, ça va?

1 **2** **3** **4**

Ça va mal.

Ça va super bien!

Comme ci comme ça.

Ça va bien.

Exemple
1 Salut Sophie, ça va?
Ça va super bien!

2 Dessine trois visages et choisis une bulle pour chacun.
Draw three faces and choose a speech bubble for each one.

Bof! Pas mal.

Ça va très mal, aujourd'hui!

Ça va très bien, merci.

3 Choisis la bonne partie du verbe 'être' et écris la bonne traduction en anglais.
Choose the correct part of the verb être and write the correct English translation.

est   suis   es   est

you are   he is   I am   she is

je _____   tu _____   il _____   elle _____

4 Complète le dialogue avec ces mots.
Complete the dialogue with these words.

pourquoi   va   fatiguée   mal   Ça   toi   va

Salut, Hugo! Ça _____?

Ça _____ bien merci, Manon. Et _____?

_____ va _____.

Ah bon _____?

Parce que je suis _____.

5 Résous les anagrammes. Associe les mots français et les mots anglais.
Solve the anagrams. Match the French words with the English words.

rsitet   étafgiu   srteéss   lmadea   esrtéses   tafegiéu

ill   *malade*   sad   _____

tired (m) _____   stressed (m) _____

tired (f) _____   stressed (f) _____

6 À deux, faites un dialogue comme celui de l'exercice 4. Utilisez les mots de l'exercice 5.
In pairs, have a conversation like the one in exercise 4. Use the words from exercise 5.

7 Choisis la bonne partie du verbe 'avoir' et écris la bonne traduction en anglais.
Choose the correct part of the verb avoir *and write the correct English translation.*

| a | as | ai | a | | you have | he has | I have | she has |

j'____   tu ____   il ____   elle ____

8 Trouve les six mots pour la famille. Écris-les avec 'mon', 'ma' ou 'mes'. Traduis en anglais.
Find the six words for members of a family. Write them with mon, ma *or* mes. *Translate into English.*

kjnfkamèreaksjdnfkdsœurldkfjltanteskdflsakfrèrelkdflskdparentsakfhoncleskdn

Exemple

1 *ma mère*   my mother

9 **a** Écoute Marie et lis les phrases. Vrai ou faux? (1–6)
Listen to Marie and read the sentences. True or false?

1 Marie thinks she has a small family.

2 Marie has two sisters.

3 Marie has two little brothers.

4 Marie's brothers are called Malik and Modou.

5 Marie's little sister is seven years old.

6 Marie's big sister is sixteen years old.

b Corrige les erreurs en anglais.
Correct the false statements in English.

Exemple

1 Faux. Marie thinks she has a big family.

10 Trouve le français pour les adjectifs. Qui est-ce?
Find the French for the adjectives. Who is it?

1 sensible   *raisonnable – Jérôme est raisonnable.*
2 kind
3 shy
4 funny
5 intelligent
6 impatient
7 chatty

Moi et ma famille

Ma mère s'appelle Hélène. Elle est petite et mince et elle a les yeux marron et les cheveux courts et noirs.
Je pense qu'elle est un peu timide mais elle est très sympa. Elle est fille unique. Mon père s'appelle Jérôme et il est mince et petit. Il n'est pas bavard – je pense qu'il est intelligent et raisonnable. Il a un frère et une sœur – mon oncle et ma tante. Mon oncle, Jean-Paul, est petit et gros et il est très drôle. Ma tante, Monique, est de taille moyenne et elle est un peu impatiente.

Salut tout le monde! Ça va? Moi, ça va bien. Je m'appelle Lucas. J'ai douze ans, je suis français et j'habite en France, à Paris, avec ma famille.

Je pense que ma famille est grande – j'ai deux sœurs et un frère. Mon frère est petit – il a neuf ans et il s'appelle Max. Il est drôle, mais il est trop bavard – il parle tout le temps! Ma petite sœur s'appelle Zoé et elle a six ans. Elle est un peu grosse, elle a les cheveux blonds et longs et je pense qu'elle est très intelligente. Ma grande sœur a les yeux bleus et les cheveux courts et blonds. Elle s'appelle Chloé, elle a dix-sept ans et elle est un peu impatiente! Moi, je suis grand et mince – je pense que je suis assez intelligent mais je suis aussi un peu paresseux.

Ma mère s'appelle Christine. Elle n'est pas grande, mais elle n'est pas petite et elle a les yeux verts et les cheveux bruns. Elle est canadienne. Elle a une grande sœur – Véronique. Véro, ma tante, habite au Canada, à Montréal, et elle a un fils qui s'appelle Hugo. Hugo, mon cousin, a douze ans comme moi, et il est super sympa. Il n'a pas de frère et il n'a pas de sœur – il est fils unique. Il parle français, mais il parle aussi anglais. Moi, je parle français et je parle anglais – un peu.

 Lis le texte. Trouve et corrige les informations fausses.
Read the text. Find and correct the false information.

1 Lucas va mal.   *Lucas va bien.*

2 Lucas a treize ans.

3 Lucas est anglais.

4 Lucas habite en Martinique.

5 Lucas habite à Marseille.

6 La famille de Lucas est petite.

7 Lucas a une sœur et un frère.

🎧2 Relis le texte et écoute la famille de Lucas. Qui parle?
Reread the text and listen to Lucas's family. Who is speaking?

Exemple

1 Lucas

✏️3 Relis le texte et regarde les images. Complète les descriptions de Véro et Hugo.
Reread the text and look at the pictures. Complete the descriptions of Véro and Hugo.

Salut! Je m'appelle Hugo.

Bonjour! Je m'appelle Véro.

4 Relis le texte et traduis les phrases.
Reread the text and translate the sentences.

1 My big sister is a bit impatient.
Ma grande sœur est un peu impatiente.

3 My little brother is funny.

5 I think I'm quite intelligent.

2 My little sister is very intelligent.

4 He is too chatty.

6 I'm a bit lazy too.

7 My cousin, Hugo, is really nice.

5 Qu'est-ce qu'il y a à Paris? Écoute Lucas et note les bonnes lettres.
What is there in Paris? Listen to Lucas and note down the correct letters.

Exemple
À Paris, il y a *f*, …

6 Regarde les images de l'exercice 5. Qu'est-ce qu'il n'y a pas à Paris? Écris trois phrases.
Look at the pictures in exercise 5. What isn't there in Paris? Write three sentences.

Exemple
À Paris, il n'y a pas de…

7 Écoute et vérifie tes réponses.
Listen and check your answers.

8 Choisis une ville. Prépare et enregistre une présentation de la ville choisie.
Choose a town. Prepare and record a presentation of your chosen town.

Rondeville

Carréville

Un festival dans notre quartier!

Use the pictures to help you work out what the friends are talking about. When you think you have a good idea of what the conversation is about, try to understand the main points in the text on the opposite page. Use a dictionary to help you.

1 AU CAFÉ ...

BONJOUR JUSTINE!

2 REGARDE, IL Y A UN FESTIVAL! MA SŒUR A DES BILLETS.

SUPER!

ET C'EST DANS LE PARC!

3 AH, TA SŒUR EST TRÈS COOL, JUSTINE!

4 ABDOU ET LA SŒUR DE JUSTINE!

5

Résumé

Les amis sont dans un café. Dans un journal, il y a une annonce pour un festival de musique dans le parc. C'est un grand festival avec des groupes de différents pays. Les amis sont très excités!

Abdou parle de la sœur de Justine. Il pense qu'elle est très cool. Les autres trouvent ça drôle.

Il y a aussi des portraits dans le journal. Mme Héros a les cheveux blonds et bouclés. Justine pense qu'elle est gentille.

L'homme s'appelle M. Vilain. Il n'est vraiment pas sympa!

Le festival est cher et Lucas pense à l'argent. Sophie a une idée...

Activité

Write a summary of the story in English. Include answers to the following questions:

- What are the friends excited about?
- Why is Lucas worried?
- What does Sophie think he should do?

Apprendre une langue – pourquoi? Why learn a language?

I speak English: why do I need to learn another language?

It's true – English is a great language to know. It has more words than any other language, it's spoken in many different places and can be very useful in all sorts of ways. So, why bother learning another language? Well, there are many different reasons – you probably know many of them already. Let's take a look, shall we?

1 Why is it good to learn another language? Work in pairs and write a list of all the reasons you can think of.

2 Try the mini-quiz below to get some more ideas.

1 How many languages are spoken around the world?

    a about 500

    b about 1000

    c almost 7000

2 How many languages are spoken in people's homes around the United Kingdom?

    a 20

    b 150

    c 300

3 What percentage of the world's population speaks no English at all?

    a 20%

    b 50%

    c 75%

3 **a** Listen to some of the quotes from young people with other reasons why it might be good to learn another language. Match what each person says with the correct symbol.

b How many of them are on your list already? Add any reasons you hadn't thought of to your list.

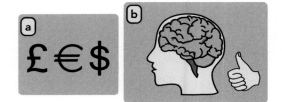

Apprendre une langue – pourquoi?

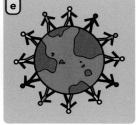

Apprendre une langue – pourquoi? Why learn French?

Your adventure into *le monde francophone* has already begun. Just think about it – you've learned quite a lot of French already. Now's a good time to put your skills to the test and also to think about why learning French is such a good idea.

LIRE, ÉCRIRE, PARLER OU COMPRENDRE LE FRANÇAIS? 200 MILLIONS DE PERSONNES AU MONDE ● 29 PAYS ONT LE FRANÇAIS COMME LANGUE OFFICIELLE ● PARLER FRANÇAIS? DANS PLUS DE 43 PAYS AU MONDE ● **LE FRANÇAIS EST LA LANGUE OFFICIELLE DE LA CROIX-ROUGE** ● LE FRANÇAIS EST UNE LANGUE OFFICIELLE DES JEUX OLYMPIQUES ● LE FRANÇAIS EST IMPORTANT DANS LE MONDE DES AFFAIRES ● LE FRANÇAIS EST IMPORTANT DANS LE MONDE DE L'ART ● **LE FRANÇAIS EST IMPORTANT DANS LE MONDE DE LA CUISINE** ● LE FRANÇAIS EST IMPORTANT DANS LE MONDE DE LA DANSE ● LE FRANÇAIS EST IMPORTANT DANS LE MONDE DE LA MODE ● LE FRANÇAIS EST LA LANGUE DE L'AMOUR ● **LE FRANÇAIS EST IMPORTANT DANS LE MONDE DE LA TECHNOLOGIE, DE LA LITTÉRATURE, DE LA RECHERCHE, DES FILMS, DES VOYAGES ... ET PLUS** ●

4 **Trouve les mots français dans le texte.**
Find the French for the following words in the text.

French	people	country	world	language	official
important	speak	read	write	understand	

5 **Relis le texte et réponds aux questions en anglais.**
Reread the text and answer the questions in English.

a In how many countries around the world is French spoken?

b How many people in the world can read, write, speak or understand French?

c How many countries have French as an official language?

6 **Regarde le texte et les images. Complète la légende pour chaque image.**
Look at the text and the pictures. Complete the caption for each picture.

1   2   3  4   5

Le français est...

7 **Trouve ou dessine une image pour illustrer la phrase numéro 2 dans le texte.**
Find or draw a picture to illustrate the second sentence of the text.

Think about how much French you've already learned – well done! Keep working hard and you'll soon know a lot more. *Bonne chance!*

À Paris, en France, il est sept heures.

À Montréal, au Canada, il est une heure.

À Hanoï, au Vietnam, il est quatorze heures.

Découverte du monde:

Do you know what time it is now in France or Canada or Martinique? Have you ever thought about what people are doing in different parts of the world while you are at school, while you are asleep, or when you get up in the morning?

Le savais-tu?

In France and other French-speaking countries people very often use the 24-hour clock. It's used to talk about timetables and people use it in general too, for example when they're talking about what time to meet up, or just telling each other what time it is. Do you know how to use the 24-hour clock?

1 **Écris les heures.**
Write the times using the 12-hour clock.

Exemple

a 15h *3 p.m.*

b 16h

c 2h

d 11h

e 21h

f 5h

g 14h

h 7h

i 12h

j 17h

2 **Parlez à deux. Quelles sont les différences entre les pays dans la vidéo et ton pays?**
Work in pairs. What are the differences between the countries you see in the video and your country?

Module 2: Ta mission...

- Describe my house
- Use regular –er verbs to describe activities at home
- Talk about my belongings
- Say where things are
- Ask and say what time it is
- Use the 24-hour clock
- Talk about a typical day, using regular –er verbs
- Use some common reflexive verbs
- Talk about school subjects
- Express opinions about school subjects
- Talk about what someone else does
- Use reflexive verbs in third person singular

Objectifs:
- Describe my house
- Use regular –er verbs to describe activities at home

Langue et grammaire

Asking what something is like

To ask what something is like, say:

C'est comment?   What's it like?

Remember to lift your voice at the end.

Using verbs

You've already seen some regular –er verbs in Module 1. In this topic you'll see several more of these. Remember, this is the pattern they follow:

manger	to eat
je mange	I eat
tu manges	you eat
il mange	he eats
elle mange	she eats
on mange	we eat

Practise these forms of all the new verbs in the *Vocabulaire* box.

Using *on*

On is a fairly informal way of saying 'we' in French and is used a lot. Look at the verb *manger* above and notice how the form of verb used with *on* is the same as the form used for *il* or *elle*.

Pronunciation

Remember not to pronounce the 's' at the end of the *tu* form of the verbs. An 's' at the end of a word is not usually pronounced in French.

---

1 **Écoute Manon, Justine, Emma et Abdou. Note qui habite à quel numéro.**

Listen to Manon, Justine, Emma and Abdou. Note down who lives at which number.

a    b    c    d

---

2 **Écoute encore. Choisis les bons mots et écris une phrase pour chaque personne.**

Listen again. Choose the correct words and write a sentence for each person.

- une petite maison
- une grande maison
- un petit appartement
- un assez grand appartement

---

3 **Parlez à deux.**

Speak in pairs.

Exemple

A Tu habites où?

B J'habite à Bristol, dans une petite maison.

A C'est comment, chez toi?

B Chez moi il y a...

Voie express

The important thing here is that you are able to use a range of –er verbs correctly, not only to say what you do yourself, but also to describe what others do. You need to know all the vocabulary for this topic and be able to use all the new verbs correctly. Exercise 6 will show how well you can do this before moving on.

4 Écoute Emma. Regarde les images et note les bonnes informations.

Listen to Emma. Look at the pictures and note down the correct information.

Exemple

d ✓, grand

a

une chambre

b

une salle à manger

c

une cuisine

d

un salon

e

une salle de bains

f

un jardin

5 Écoute et associe les deux parties de chaque phrase.
Listen and match the two parts of each sentence.

Vocabulaire	
une maison	a house
un appartement	a flat
une cuisine	a kitchen
une chambre	a bedroom
une salle de bains	a bathroom
une salle à manger	a dining room
un salon	a living room
un jardin	a garden
manger	to eat
habiter	to live
regarder	to watch
jouer	to play
chanter	to sing
écouter	to listen
partager	to share
une tablette	a tablet
Quelle horreur!	How awful!
Quel dommage!	What a pity!
chez moi/toi	(at) my/your house
à tour de role	in turn
chacun	each
avec	with

1 Dans le salon

2 Dans la cuisine

3 Dans la salle de bains

4 Dans ma chambre

a on regarde la télé.

b je parle avec ma sœur ou je joue sur ma tablette.

c on mange – parce qu'il n'y a pas de salle à manger.

d ma mère chante!

6 Remplis les blancs pour Abdou.
Fill the blanks for Abdou.

chambres   regarde   mange   parle   partage   jardin   joue   écoute

Chez moi il y a trois **1** _____. Je **2** _____ une chambre avec mon grand frère. Dans ma chambre je **3** _____ sur ma tablette ou je **4** _____ avec mon frère. Il y a aussi un salon. On **5** _____ la télé dans le salon et on **6** _____ dans la salle à manger. Il y a une petite cuisine – dans la cuisine mon père **7** _____ la radio. Il n'y a pas de **8** _____.

7 C'est comment chez toi? Décris où tu habites.
What is your house like? Describe where you live. Include as much detail as you can.

Objectifs
- Talk about my belongings
- Say where things are

Langue et grammaire

Using prepositions

Prepositions are used to talk about where things are. They're easy to use.

Dans ma chambre… — In my bedroom…

Ma guitare est sous le lit. — My guitar is under the bed.

Ma guitare est sur le lit. — My guitar is on the bed.

Ma guitare est derrière la porte. — My guitar is behind the door.

The indefinite article and the definite article

The indefinite article in English is 'a' or 'an'. In French, use:

un for a masculine noun   *un lit*   a bed
une for a feminine noun   *une porte*   a door
des for a plural noun   *des étagères*   some shelves

The definite article in English is 'the'. In French, use:

le for a masculine noun   *le lit*   the bed
la for a feminine noun   *la porte*   the door
les for a plural noun   *les lits*   the beds

Pronunciation

Practise how to pronounce *sur* and *sous* so you don't get them mixed up. Push your lips forward into a pout for *sous*.

Notice how words ending in *–able* are pronounced differently in French. For example, *un portable*. Accents change the pronunciation of the letter 'e'. Listen carefully to the word *étagère*. What other words do you know containing é or è?

---

 1 **Écoute. Écris les lettres dans l'ordre et choisis le bon symbole.**

Listen. Write the letters in the correct order and choose the correct symbol.

 j'aime j'adore

a	b	c	d	e	f

une guitare   un ballon de basket   un portable   une montre   une trottinette   un portefeuille

Exemple **d**

 2 **Écoute encore et choisis la bonne raison pour chaque réponse de l'exercice 1.**

Listen again and write a reason for each answer in exercise 1.

jolie   cool   moderne   pratique   génial

Exemple **d** 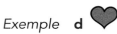 parce qu'elle est cool

 3 **Écris des phrases pour décrire tes affaires.**

Write some sentences to describe some of your belongings.

Exemple   J'ai une montre. J'aime ma montre parce qu'elle est cool et très moderne.

Voie express

You need to know when to use 'the' and when to use 'a/an/some' and be able to use a range of 'position' words, or prepositions. Draw a picture of your dream room with all your favourite things in it. Write a paragraph describing where your favourite things are and explain why you like them.

4 Écoute. Qu'est-ce qu'Abdou a dans sa chambre?
Écris les lettres dans le bon ordre. (1–6)

Listen. What does Abdou have in his bedroom?
Write the letters in the order you hear them.

> Dans ma chambre j'ai 1_____, j'ai 2_____, j'ai aussi 3_____. J'ai 4_____, un 5 _____ et bien sûr, il y a 6_____.

a   un tapis

b   un lit

c   une chaise

d   une table

e   une porte

f   une étagère

Vocabulaire

les affaires	belongings
un portable	a mobile phone
un ballon de basket	a basketball
une trottinette	a scooter
une montre	a watch
une guitare	a guitar
un portefeuille	a wallet
un lit	a bed
une porte	a door
une étagère	a shelf
une table	a table
un tapis	a rug
un pouf-poire	a beanbag
un ordinateur	a computer
une chaise	a chair
une armoire	a wardrobe
moderne	modern
pratique	practical
aimer	to like
adorer	to love
sous	under, underneath
sur	over, on top
derrière	behind

5 À deux parlez de vos chambres.

In pairs talk about your bedrooms.

A Qu'est-ce que tu as dans ta chambre?
B Dans ma chambre j'ai…

6 Où sont les objets? Vrai ou faux?

Where are all the things? True or false?

1 Ma guitare est sur le lit.

2 Ma montre est derrière le pouf-poire.

3 Mon portefeuille est sur l'étagère.

4 Ma trottinette est derrière la porte.

5 Mon ballon de basket est sur la table.

6 Mon portable est sous le tapis.

7 Mon ordinateur est sur la table.

7 Où sont les objets? Écris les phrases vraies.

Where are all the things? Write true sentences for the items above that were false.

8 Dessine ta chambre et tes affaires.
Écris une description.

Draw your bedroom and your belongings. Write a description.

Objectifs
- Ask and say what time it is
- Use the 24-hour clock

Langue et grammaire

Telling the time

To say what time it is, use the phrase *Il est...*

Il est cinq heures.	It's five o'clock.
Il est deux heures dix.	It's ten past two.
Il est huit heures moins cinq.	It's five to eight.
Il est cinq heures et quart.	It's quarter past five.
Il est neuf heures moins le quart.	It's quarter to nine.
Il est deux heures et demie.	It's half past two.

When it's one o'clock, the word *heure* is singular so it is spelled without an 's'.

Il est une heure.

The 24-hour clock is very often used in France and around the world:

Il est dix heures.	It's 10 a.m.
Il est quinze heures.	It's 3 p.m.

If you want to use the 12-hour clock in French, use the phrases *du matin* and *du soir*:

Il est huit heures du matin.	It's eight o'clock in the morning.
Il est neuf heures du soir.	It's nine o'clock in the evening.

Questions

The word *quel(le)* is used to ask 'what' or 'which'. When you ask a question using *quel(le)*, you swap the positions of the subject and the verb, like this:

Quelle heure est-il?	What time is it?

Notice the hyphen in *est-il*.

Pronunciation

In French, the letters 'oi' are pronounced 'wa', like in the word *moi*.

---

1 Écoute et écris les chiffres.

Listen and write down the numbers you hear. What pattern can you see?

Vocabulaire

un(e) correspondant(e)	penpal
un(e) ami(e)	friend
possible	possible
moins	to when telling time, or less/minus
moins le quart	a quarter to
et quart	a quarter past
(et) demie	half past
appeler	to call (by phone)

2 **a Jouez à deux. Lisez les chiffres.**

In pairs take turns to say the numbers in French, then swap over.

5	10	15	20	25	30
35	40	45	50	55	60

b Maintenant, comptez par deux, par trois et par quatre de zéro à soixante.

Now try counting in twos, threes and fours from 0 to 60.

3 **À deux, regardez les images. Quelle heure est-il?**

In pairs, look at the pictures. What time is it?

Exemple

A Image c. Quelle heure est-il?

B Il est cinq heures trente.

a 11:10

b  09:05

c 05:30

d 15:20

e 19:05

f 2:25

g 06:50

h 00:15

4 Regarde l'image et écoute les conversations. Qui peut faire l'appel?
Look at the picture and listen to the conversations. Who can make a call?

À Manchester   À Paris

À Montréal   10h   À Hanoï

05h   11h

À Montréal

10h   17h

05h   À Nouméa

À Saint-Pierre   14h   22h

À Dakar   À Antananarivo

c'est la nuit   c'est le matin   c'est l'après-midi   c'est le soir

Lucas   Sophie

Maeva   Abdou

5 Regarde encore l'image de l'exercice 4 et écris une réponse pour chaque personne.
Look at the picture in exercise 5 and write an answer for each person.

1
J'appelle Marie à Dakar sur Skype, d'accord?

Abdou
Paris, France

2
J'appelle Emma à Saint-Pierre sur Skype, d'accord?

Manon
Paris, France

3
J'appelle mon correspondant à Nouméa sur Skype, d'accord?

Félix
Paris, France

4
J'appelle ma correspondant à Antananarivo sur Skype, d'accord?

Sophie
Paris, France

Les numéros

vingt et un	twenty-one
vingt-deux	twenty-two
vingt-trois	twenty-three
vingt-quatre	twenty-four
vingt-cinq	twenty-five
vingt-six	twenty-six
vingt-sept	twenty-seven
vingt-huit	twenty-eight
vingt-neuf	twenty-nine
trente	thirty
quarante	forty
cinquante	fifty
soixante	sixty
le matin	morning
l'après-midi	afternoon
le soir	evening

6 À deux. Chacun demande et dit l'heure pour chaque ville. Puis écris les réponses.
In pairs. Each asks and gives the time for each place. Then write your answers.

Quand il est seize heures à Paris, quelle heure est-il à...

1 Hanoï?   **2** Saint-Pierre?

3 Dakar?   **4** Nouméa?

5 Antananarivo? **6** Manchester?

Voie express

Numbers up to 60 are essential for telling the time. Each set of ten numbers from 20 to 60 follows the same pattern. Learn the numbers 20, 30, 40, 50 and 60, then the numbers in between are quicker to learn.

Objectifs
- Talk about a typical day, using regular –er verbs
- Use some common reflexive verbs

Langue et grammaire

Using reflexive verbs

A reflexive verb is just the same as any other verb, but also has a small word called a reflexive pronoun which comes before it. These sorts of verbs are often actions that you do to yourself.

je **me** lève	I get up
tu **te** lèves	you get up
il **se** lève	he gets up
elle **se** lève	she gets up
on **se** lève	we get up

The reflexive pronoun is shortened when it comes before a vowel or before the silent *h*:

je **m'**habille	I get dressed

Saying what time you do something

Use the preposition *à* to say what time you do something:

Tu te lèves à quelle heure?	What time do you get up?
Je me lève à huit heures.	I get up at eight o'clock.

Negatives

To say that you never do something, use *ne ... jamais* around the verb. Note that the reflexive pronoun is included inside the *ne ... jamais*:

*Je **ne** joue **jamais** dans le jardin.*	I never play in the garden.
*Je **ne** me lève **jamais** à six heures.*	I never get up at six o'clock.

1 Regarde les images et écoute Sophie. Écris les lettres dans le bon ordre.

Look at the pictures and listen to Sophie. Write the letters in the correct order.

a	b	c	d	e	f

2 Écoute Sophie encore et écris en chiffres l'heure pour chaque réponse.

Listen to Sophie again and write the correct time in numbers for each answer.

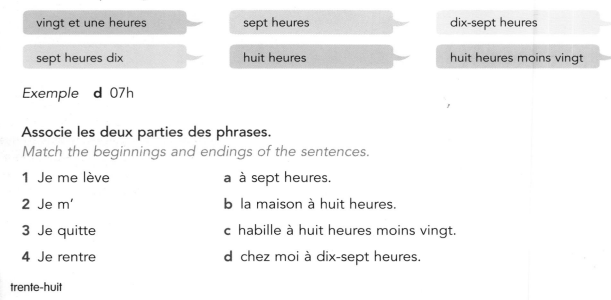

vingt et une heures	sept heures	dix-sept heures
sept heures dix	huit heures	huit heures moins vingt

Exemple **d** 07h

3 Associe les deux parties des phrases.

Match the beginnings and endings of the sentences.

1 Je me lève		**a**	à sept heures.
2 Je m'		**b**	la maison à huit heures.
3 Je quitte		**c**	habille à huit heures moins vingt.
4 Je rentre		**d**	chez moi à dix-sept heures.

4 Thomas écris son blog. Choisis la/les bonne(s) image(s) pour chaque jour.

Thomas is writing his blog. Choose the correct picture(s) for each day. Hint: Quelle semaine de galère! means 'What a terrible week!'

Monday   *c*

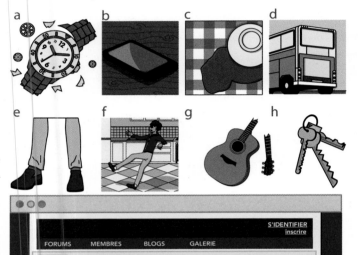

Vocabulaire

se lever	to get up
se laver	to have a wash
s'habiller	to get dressed
quitter la maison	to leave the house
rentrer (chez moi)	to go home
se coucher	to go to bed
trouver	to find
rater	to miss (the bus)
tomber	to fall
renverser	to spill
oublier	to forget
casser	to break
le petit-déjeuner	breakfast
le chocolat chaud	hot chocolate
les clés	keys
lundi	Monday
mardi	Tuesday
mercredi	Wednesday
jeudi	Thursday
vendredi	Friday
samedi	Saturday
dimanche	Sunday
vers	around
la semaine	week

S'IDENTIFIER
inscrire

FORUMS   MEMBRES   BLOGS   GALERIE

Mon Blog
Posté par **Thomas** 18 juin 15:25

Quelle semaine de galère! Lundi, je renverse mon chocolat chaud. Mardi, je rate le bus. Mercredi, j'oublie mon portable. Jeudi, je tombe dans la cuisine et je casse ma montre. Vendredi, quand je rentre chez moi, je ne trouve pas mes clés. Samedi, je rate le bus – encore! Et dimanche... je reste dans mon lit!!!

Oh Thomas, c'est vrai – quelle semaine de galère! Moi, je ne renverse jamais mon chocolat chaud. Je...

5 Sophie lit le blog de Thomas. Complète les phrases avec *ne … jamais*. Puis traduis en anglais.

Sophie is reading Thomas's blog. Complete the sentences using ne … jamais. *Then translate into English.*

1 Je _____ renverse _____ mon chocolat chaud.

2 Je _____ rate _____ le bus.

3 Je _____ oublie _____ mon portable.

4 Je _____ tombe _____.

5 Je _____ casse _____ ma montre.

Voie express

Reflexive verbs are common and it is important that you know how to use them. Prepare a presentation about your daily routine, saying what time you usually do things. Also mention the things you never do.

6 Écris une réponse à Thomas. Décris une semaine typique. ⭐

Write a reply to Thomas. Describe a typical week.

Objectifs
- Talk about school subjects
- Express opinions about school subjects

Langue et grammaire

Talking about school subjects

To talk about what subjects you have on a particular day, use the verb *avoir* **without** *le/la/les*:

Lundi, j'ai français.	On Monday, I have French.
Mardi, il a maths.	On Tuesday, he has maths.
Vendredi, elle a sciences.	On Friday, she has science.
Jeudi, on a géographie.	On Thursday, we have geography.

To talk about which school subjects you like or don't like, use the word for the school subject **with** the definite article (*le/la/les*):

J'aime le français.   I like French.

Days of the week

Days of the week are written without a capital letter unless they begin a sentence.

Lundi, j'ai maths et	On Monday, I have maths and
mardi, j'ai français.	on Tuesday, I have French.

Pronunciation

Notice how the letters of the alphabet are pronounced differently in French. For example, *EPS* is pronouned 'euh pay ess'.

---

 1 **Écoute et écris le bon jour et les bonnes lettres. (1–3)**
Listen and write the day and the correct letters.

Exemple **1** mardi – d, f, ...

a   b   c

d    e   f

g   h   i

Vocabulaire

les maths (f)	maths
les sciences (f)	science
l'histoire (f)	history
l'EPS (f)	PE
le théâtre	drama
l'informatique (f)	ICT
les arts plastiques	art
la technologie	technology
la musique	music
intéressant(e)	interesting
ennuyeux(–euse)	boring
facile	easy
difficile	difficult
la matière	subject
détester	to hate
beaucoup	a lot

---

2 **Regardez les réponses à l'exercice 1. À deux, parlez de Lucas.**
Look at the answers to exercise 1. In pairs, speak about Lucas.

Exemple

A C'est mardi. Lucas a quelles matières aujourd'hui?
B Il a ..., il a ...

---

3 **Fais un sondage. Pose les questions à 10 personnes. Note les réponses.**
Do a survey. Ask 10 people if they like a subject and why. Record the replies in a table.

4

Lis les bulles. Vrai ou faux?
Read the bubbles. True or false?

a J'aime l'anglais et j'adore la musique et l'EPS – c'est amusant. Mais je n'aime pas le théâtre. C'est ennuyeux.

b J'aime beaucoup l'histoire mais je n'aime pas le français parce que c'est difficile, et je déteste les arts plastiques.

c J'adore les sciences et les maths, mais je n'aime pas beaucoup l'histoire. C'est nul.

d J'aime beaucoup la géographie parce que c'est intéressant, mais je déteste les maths.

e J'adore l'anglais, j'adore l'histore et j'adore le français. C'est facile.

f J'aime l'informatique. C'est cool. Mais je déteste l'EPS et la technologie.

1 Abdou loves PE.

2 Félix doesn't like French.

3 Justine loves science.

4 Maeva likes maths.

5 Sophie hates English.

6 Lucas hates DT.

7 Abdou thinks drama is difficult.

8 Félix thinks French is boring.

9 Justine thinks history is rubbish.

10 Maeva thinks geography is interesting.

11 Sophie thinks French is easy.

12 Lucas thinks ICT is boring.

5

Relis l'exercice 4 et réponds en français.
Reread exercise 4 and reply in French.

1 Qui adore l'anglais?   *Sophie*

2 Qui aime l'informatique?

3 Qui déteste les arts plastiques?

4 Qui déteste les maths?

5 Qui n'aime pas l'histoire, mais adore les sciences?

6 Qui n'aime pas le théâtre mais adore la musique?

6

Écris un paragraphe pour décrire les matières que tu aimes et n'aimes pas.
Write a paragraph about the subjects you like and don't like.

Exemple   J'adore ... parce que c'est...

            Je n'aime pas ... parce que c'est...

Voie express

You need to know the vocabulary for the main subjects that you learn at school and be able to give reasons for your opinions about them. Being able to justify your opinions about all sorts of things is an important language skill. Think of some more reasons why you might like or dislike a school subject and use a dictionary to find out what these are in French. Choose two days of the week and write about what you study on those days, whether you enjoy those subjects or not and why.

Objectifs
- Talk about what someone else does
- Use reflexive verbs in third person singular

Langue et grammaire

Talking about what someone else does

To talk about what another person does, use the third person singular of a verb (the form we use for 'he' or 'she'). It is the same form that you have been using with *on*. Look at these examples:

Il quitte la maison.	He leaves the house.
Elle regarde la télé.	She watches TV.
Il fait ses devoirs.	He does homework.

Remember that reflexive verbs have a reflexive pronoun before the verb:

Je me lève.	I get up.
Il se couche.	He goes to bed.
Elle s'habille.	She gets dressed.

1 **Lis les e-mails et choisis les bons mots pour compléter les phrases.**
Read the emails and chose the correct words to complete the sentences.

> Salut Antoine! Ça va?
>
> C'est drôle! Quand je me lève à sept heures, ici à Paris, tu rentres à la maison. Et le mardi matin à onze heures, quand j'ai EPS, tu te couches!
>
> À bientôt – Fabrice

> Salut Fabrice! Ça va bien merci.
>
> C'est vrai – c'est drôle! Le mardi matin, quand je quitte la maison à sept heures ici à Nouméa tu te couches – et c'est toujours lundi à Paris!
> C'est amusant – il y a dix heures de différence!
>
> À bientôt – Antoine

gets up	goes to bed	goes home	fine	goes to bed	ten	leaves the house

1 Antoine says he's _____.

2 Fabrice _____ at seven o'clock.

3 When Fabrice gets up Antoine _____.

4 Antoine _____ at seven o'clock.

5 Fabrice has PE when Antoine _____.

6 Antoine leaves the house when Fabrice _____.

7 There is a _____ -hour time difference between France and New Caledonia.

2 **Associe les deux parties des phrases pour traduire les phrases anglaises.**
Match the two parts of the sentences to translate the English sentences.

1 He gets up at seven o'clock.

2 He leaves the house at eight o'clock.

3 He has PE at eleven o'clock.

4 He gets dressed at seven thirty.

5 He goes to bed at nine o'clock.

6 He does homework at seven in the evening.

1 Il se couche	a à onze heures.
2 Il s'habille	b à huit heures.
3 Il se lève	c à dix-neuf heures.
4 Il fait ses devoirs	d à sept heures.
5 Il a EPS	e à vingt et une heures.
6 Il quitte la maison	f à sept heures trente.

3 Écoute les informations et remplis les blancs pour Maeva et pour Luyen.

Listen to the information and fill in the blanks for Maeva and for Luyen.

J'ai un e-mail de ma correspondante, Luyen, à Hanoï, au Vietnam. C'est cool – quand je me lève à 1_____ heures ici à Paris, elle 2_____ et il est 3_____ à Hanoï. Quand j'ai maths à quatorze heures, elle 4_____ et il est vingt et une heures à Hanoï. Et quand elle 5_____ à sept heures, je suis toujours dans mon lit.

J'ai un e-mail de ma correspondante, Maeva, à Paris, en France. C'est cool – quand j'ai anglais à quatorze heures ici à Hanoï, elle 6_____ , et quand 7_____ à quinze heures, elle 8_____ . À dix-sept heures je rentre chez moi et elle 9_____ et à vingt et une heures à Paris elle 10_____ et je suis déjà dans mon lit.

4 Parlez à deux. A pose les questions. B répond. A note les réponses.

Work in pairs. A asks the questions. B replies. A notes their replies. Then swap roles.

1 Tu te lèves à quelle heure?

2 Tu quittes la maison à quelle heure?

3 Tu as français à quelle heure?

4 Tu rentres à quelle heure?

5 Tu te couches à quelle heure?

5 Écris un paragraphe qui décrit la journée de ton partenaire.

Now write a paragraph describing your partner's day.

Exemple

Sophie se lève à sept heures. Elle quitte la maison…

Vocabulaire

une différence	a difference
ici	here
la Nouvelle-Calédonie	New Caledonia
à bientôt	see you soon
toujours	still, always
déjà	already
donc	so
faire ses devoirs	to do homework
je fais mes devoirs	I do homework
il/elle fait ses devoirs	he/she does homework

Langue et grammaire

Asking what something is like

To ask what something is like say:
C'est comment?   What's it like?

Using *on* to mean 'we'

On is an informal way of saying 'we'. Use the same form of verb as for 'he' or 'she'.

Using prepositions

Use prepositions to talk about where things are.
Ma guitare est sous le lit. My guitar is under the bed.

The indefinite article and the definite article

In French there are three words for 'a' or 'an':

un for a masculine noun	*un lit*	a bed
une for a feminine noun	*une porte*	a door
des for a plural noun	*des amis*	some friends

There are also three words for 'the':

le for a masculine noun	*le lit*	the bed
la for a feminine noun	*la porte*	the door
les for a plural noun	*les lits*	the beds

Telling the time

To tell the time, use the phrase *Il est.*

Il est cinq heures.	It's five o'clock.
Il est deux heures dix.	It's ten past two.
Il est huit heures moins cinq.	It's five to eight.

Il est cinq heures et quart.	It's quarter past five.
Il est une heure moins le quart.	It's quarter to one.
Il est deux heures et demie.	It's half past two.

The 24-hour clock is very often used in France:

Il est quinze heures.	It's 3 p.m.

If you want to use the 12-hour clock in French, use the phrases *du matin* and *du soir.*

Il est huit heures du matin.	It's 8 a.m.
Il est neuf heures du soir.	It's 9 p.m.

Questions

Quel(le) is used to ask 'what' or 'which'. When you ask a question using *quel(le)*, you swap the positions of the subject and the verb, like this:
Quelle heure est-il?   What time is it?

Using reflexive verbs

A reflexive verb is just the same as any other verb, but also has a small word called a reflexive pronoun which comes before it.

je me lève	I get up
tu te lèves	you get up
il/elle se lève	he/she gets up
on se lève	we get up

Asking and saying what time you do something

Use the preposition *à* to say what time you do something:
Je me lève à huit heures. I get up at eight o'clock.

Negatives

To say that you never do something, put *ne ... jamais* around the verb:

Je ne rate jamais le bus.	I never miss the bus.
Je ne me lève jamais à 6h.	I never get up at 6 a.m.

Talking about school subjects

To talk about what subjects you have, use *avoir* and the word for the subject without the definite article (*le/la/les*):
Lundi, j'ai français.   On Monday, I have French.

To talk about which subjects you like or don't like, use the word for the subject with the definite article (*le/la/les*):

J'aime le français.	I like French.
Je n'aime pas les maths.	I don't like maths.
J'adore la géographie.	I love geography.

Talking about what someone else does

To talk about what another person does, use the third person singular of a verb (the form used for 'he' or 'she').

Il quitte la maison.	He leaves the house.
Sophie quitte la maison.	Sophie leaves the house.

Vocabulaire

À la maison
la maison
l'appartement (m)
la cuisine
la chambre
la salle de bains
la salle à manger
le salon
le jardin

Les verbes courants
manger
habiter
regarder
jouer
chanter
écouter
partager
aimer
adorer
détester
appeler

Mes affaires
le portable
le ballon de basket

la trottinette
la montre
la guitare
le portefeuille
le lit
la porte
l'étagère (f)
la table
le tapis
le pouf-poire
l'ordinateur (m)
la chaise
l'armoire (f)
la tablette
les clés

Les numéros
vingt
vingt et un
vingt-deux
vingt-trois etc.
trente
trente et un
trente-deux
trente-trois etc.
quarante
quarante et un

quarante-deux
quarante-trois etc.
cinquante
cinquante et un
cinquante-deux
cinquante-trois etc.
soixante

L'heure
moins cinq
moins le quart
et quart
(et) demie
le matin
l'après-midi
le soir

Les jours
lundi
mardi
mercredi
jeudi
vendredi
samedi
dimanche

Les adjectifs
intéressant(e)
ennuyeux(–euse)
facile
difficile
moderne
pratique

La vie quotidienne
se lever
se laver
s'habiller
se coucher
quitter la maison
rentrer (chez moi/ toi)
trouver
rater
tomber
renverser
oublier
casser
faire ses devoirs
le petit-déjeuner
le chocolat chaud
boulot

Les matières
la matière
le théâtre
l'informatique (f)
les arts plastiques (m)
la technologie
la musique

Les mots utiles
Quelle horreur!
Quel dommage!
ici
vers
sous
beaucoup
déjà
donc
à bientôt
toujours
un(e) correspondant(e)
un(e) ami(e)
possible
sur
derrière
chacun
la différence

Mission accomplie?

I can...

Describe my house
Use regular –er verbs to describe activities at home
Talk about my belongings
Say where things are
Ask and say what time it is
Use the 24-hour clock
Talk about a typical day, using regular –er verbs
Use some common reflexive verbs
Talk about school subjects
Express opinions about school subjects
Talk about what someone else does
Use reflexive verbs in third person singular

1

a Regarde les images, trouve les verbes et choisis la bonne pièce pour compléter les phrases.

Look at the pictures, find the verbs and choose the correct room from the list to complete the sentences.

a **b** **c** **d**

e **f** **g**

é	l	p	r	j	d	b	r
u	c	é	c	o	u	t	e
q	h	g	l	u	a	h	g
m	a	n	g	e	n	a	a
w	n	y	e	j	a	b	r
e	t	i	h	n	m	i	d
z	e	l	s	z	h	t	e
p	a	r	t	a	g	e	t

une chambre · la cuisine · la salle de bains · le salon
le jardin · la salle à manger · une petite maison

1 *J'habite* dans *une petite maison.* **2** Je _____ la télé dans _____.

3 Je _____ dans _____. **4** Je _____ avec ma sœur.

5 Je _____ dans _____. **6** Je _____ dans _____.

7 J'_____ la radio dans _____.

b Traduis les phrases en anglais.

Now translate the sentences into English.

2 Remplis les blancs avec 'mon' ou 'ma'.

Fill the gaps with mon *or* ma.

1 J'ai une montre – j'aime _____ montre. **2** J'ai un portefeuille – j'aime _____ portefeuille.

3 J'ai un portable – j'adore _____ portable. **4** J'ai une trottinette – j'aime _____ trottinette.

5 J'ai une guitare – j'adore _____ guitare. **6** J'ai un ballon de basket – j'adore _____ ballon de basket.

3 Sépare les mots pour traduire les phrases 1–3, puis traduis les phrases 4–6.

Separate the words to translate sentences 1–3, then translate sentences 4–6.

1 I like my watch because it's cool. **2** I like my wallet because it's practical.

3 I love my basketball because it's fun. **4** I like my scooter because it's really cool.

5 I love my guitar because it's beautiful. **6** I love my mobile phone because it's modern.

Jaimemamontreparcequecestcool.   Jaimemonportefeuilleparcequecestpratique.   Jadoremonballondebasketparcequecestamusant.

4 **a Réponds aux questions.**

Answer the questions.

1 Qui est sur Félix?

2 Qui est derrière Lucas?

3 Qui est sous Abdou?

b Remplis les blancs avec les prépositions de la partie a.

Fill the gaps with the prepositions in part a.

1 Abdou est _____ Lucas.

2 Félix est _____ Thomas.

3 Justine est _____ Sophie.

Thomas
Félix, Manon, Maeva
Lucas, Abdou, Justine, Sophie

5 **Écris l'heure et choisis la bonne description pour chaque image.**

Write the time and choose the correct description for each picture.

1 **14:00** 2 **07:00** 3 **19:00** 4 **23:00** 5 **03:00** 6 **16:00**

C'est le matin.   C'est l'après-midi.   C'est le soir.   C'est la nuit.

Exemple

1 Il est quatorze heures. C'est l'après-midi.

6 **Écoute les phrases françaises et remplis les blancs en anglais.**

Listen to the French sentences and fill in the gaps in English.

1 I <u>get up</u> at six o'clock.

2 I _____ my breakfast.

3 I _____ in my bedroom.

4 I _____ at eight o'clock.

5 I _____ at five o'clock.

6 I _____ at ten o'clock.

7 **Vrai ou faux?**

True or false?

a Tomorrow is Wednesday.

b Thomas loves Tuesdays.

c He has music and French in the afternoon.

d He has science and maths in the morning.

e He thinks maths is boring.

Aujourd'hui c'est mardi. Je n'aime pas le mardi! Le matin on a théâtre, sciences et maths et l'après-midi on a français et musique. Je n'aime pas le théâtre – je pense que c'est nul. Je déteste le français parce que c'est difficile et la musique – je pense que c'est ennuyeux. J'aime les maths mais c'est un peu difficile et les sciences – bof!

2

1

a Dans le e-mail trouve le français pour ces phrases.

In the email find the French for these sentences.

1 I love Wednesdays.

2 There's no school.

3 My sister doesn't like mornings.

4 We leave the house at eight o'clock.

À: Tiana

Salut Tiana!

C'est mercredi! J'adore le mercredi parce que, l'après-midi, ici à Paris, il n'y a pas de collège! Je me lève à sept heures, je m'habille et je mange mon petit-déjeuner avec ma sœur à sept heures vingt. Ma sœur n'aime pas le matin – elle est fatiguée donc elle n'est pas contente. On quitte la maison à huit heures. Le mercredi j'ai anglais, maths et technologie. Je rentre chez moi à onze heures cinquante et l'après-midi je joue avec mes copains. Et pour toi, à Antananarivo, le mercredi est comment?

À bientôt, Sophie

b Quelle image représente le mercredi pour Sophie?

Which picture represents Wednesdays for Sophie?

c Choisis la bonne heure pour chaque activité.

Choose the correct time for each activity.

1
2
3

a 09:00
b 07:20
c
d 11:50
e 08:00

d Mets les mots dans le bon ordre pour répondre aux questions en français.
Put the words in the correct order to reply to the questions in French.
Hint: sa and ses mean 'her'.

1 What time does Sophie get up?

à heures elle sept lève se

2 Who does she eat breakfast with?

mange petit-déjeuner avec le sœur
sa elle

3 Does she get dressed at 10 o'clock?

s'habille non à heures cinq elle sept

4 What does she do on Wednesday afternoons?

joue avec elle copains ses

[2] Lis le e-mail. Écris une liste de tous les verbes. Associe ces verbes avec la bonne phrase anglaise.
Read the email. Write a list of all the verbs. Match them with the correct English phrase.

Exemple
j'ai I have

I like
you don't have
we sing
I go home
I love
I don't play
I watch
I listen to
I don't play
I think
I hate
I go to bed
I eat

À: Sophie

Salut Sophie!
Ah, quelle chance – tu n'as pas de collège le mercredi après-midi! Moi, j'ai collège lundi, mardi, mercredi, jeudi, vendredi ET samedi matin! J'aime beaucoup mon collège mais j'adore le samedi après-midi et le dimanche. Le samedi matin j'ai musique, anglais et sciences. Je déteste l'anglais parce que je pense que c'est difficile mais j'adore la musique parce qu'on chante et je pense que c'est cool. Et les sciences – bof! Le mercredi je rentre chez moi à dix-sept heures et je ne joue pas avec mes copains ... je mange avec ma famille, je regarde la télé ou j'écoute la radio et je me couche à vingt et une heures.
À bientôt, Tiana

[3] Relis le e-mail et écoute. Vrai ou faux? (1–9)
Reread the email and listen. Write true or false.

[4] Écris un e-mail et décris un jour de la semaine que tu aimes ou que tu n'aimes pas. Utilise ces titres:
Write an email and describe a day of the week that you like or don't like. Use these headings:

1 Ma routine le matin (My morning routine)

2 Les matières que j'aime et que je n'aime pas, et pourquoi! (Subjects that I like and dislike, and why!)

3 Ma routine le soir (My evening routine)

Le boulot idéal

Use the pictures to help you work out what Lucas is doing. Can you guess the meaning of the word boulot? Look it up in a dictionary or in the glossary of this book to find out if you were right.

1 DANS LA CHAMBRE DE LUCAS...

BOF! JE NE TROUVE JAMAIS DE BOULOT. C'EST TROP DIFFICILE. J'APPELLE MES AMIS.

2

TIENS, UN BOULOT DANS UN MAGASIN.

ALORS LUCAS, QU'EST-CE QUE TU AIMES FAIRE?

NON! JE N'AIME PAS LES MATHS.

D'ACCORD... DANS UN RESTAURANT?

QUELLE HORREUR!

BOF... J'AIME ALLER AU PARC... ET J'ADORE LA MUSIQUE...

3 Offres d'emploi

livreur
3 heures par
emplois@pizzapalais.fr

EH BIEN, C'EST PARFAIT!

jardinier
2 heures samedi matin
M. Dupont du.p@frmail.fr

ouvrier agricol
Du lundi au vend
fermierjoe@haut

BON! J'APPELLE CE SOIR.

4

D'ACCORD, CHEZ MOI À QUINZE HEURES TRENTE?

SUPER! MERCI!

5 IL EST DIX-SEPT HEURES TRENTE.

LUCAS N'EST PAS FATIGUÉ...

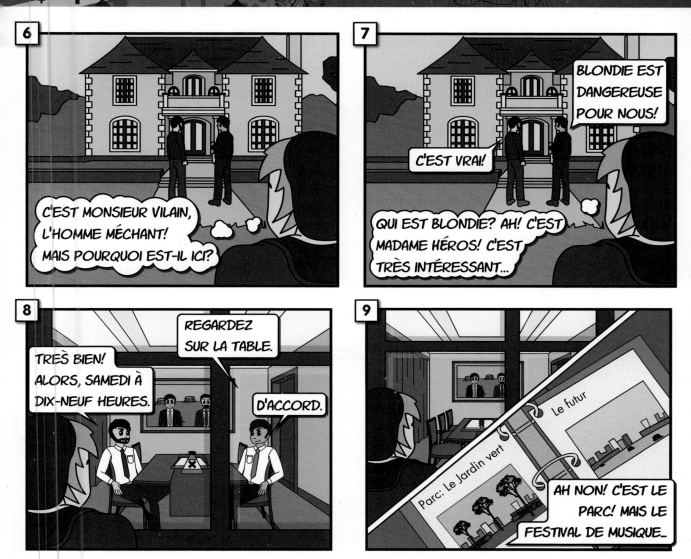

Résumé

Lucas est sur son ordi. Il regarde les *Offres d'emploi*, mais il ne trouve pas de boulot. Il est fatigué, donc il appelle Félix et Maeva pour l'aider. Maeva propose des boulots, mais Lucas est très difficile! Il n'aime pas les maths et il n'aime pas travailler dans un restaurant. Maeva demande «Alors Lucas, tu aimes quoi?»

Lucas pense… Il aime être dans le jardin et il adore écouter de la musique. Ils trouvent un boulot dans le jardin d'un homme qui s'appelle Monsieur Dupont. Lucas appelle le numéro dans l'offre d'emploi. L'appel se passe bien et le boulot commence cet après-midi.

Le boulot est facile. Lucas fait le jardinage et écoute sa musique – c'est parfait! Mais pourquoi est-ce que Monsieur Vilain est là? Il parle de Madame Héros avec Monsieur Dupont. Lucas écoute. Ils disent qu'elle est dangereuse. Ils ont un rendez-vous samedi à dix-neuf heures. Dans le bureau, Lucas voit des plans pour transformer le parc en parking. Il est horrifié! C'est son parc préféré, et le site du festival aussi!

Activité

Sketch out some panels for a comic strip about you and your friends.

- Think about what your characters are like.

- Include a simple conversation in French.

- Try to make it funny!

Using a dictionary

A dictionary can be very useful when you're learning a language. There are different types of dictionary – monolingual dictionaries (written in only one language) or bilingual dictionaries (with translations from one language into another).

It's likely that you'll be using a bilingual dictionary at the moment. How much do you know about when it's a good idea to use a dictionary, how bilingual dictionaries are organised and what information you can find out by using one?

1 **Regarde un dictionnaire français. À deux, répondez aux questions.**
Look at a French dictionary. In pairs, answer the questions.

équipe *nf* <u>team</u>

crier *vb* <u>to shout</u>

1 Should you look in the front or back half of the dictionary to find out the meaning of a French word?

2 Should you look in the front or back half of the dictionary to find out how to say an English word in French?

3 What order do the words appear in?

4 How can the words at the top of each page help you?

5 Look at the examples above. Apart from a translation, what other information is provided about each word?

6 Are there any other sections in the dictionary you are using? What are they for?

2 **Écrivez les deux listes dans l'ordre alphabétique.**
Write these two lists in alphabetical order.

3 **Dans le dictionnaire cherche le mot français pour chaque image. Écris le mot et choisis la bonne classification.**
In the dictionary find the French word for each picture. Write the word and say whether it is masculine or feminine, singular or plural.

Prénoms	Pays francophones
Justine	Martinique
Lucas	Monaco
Abdou	Maroc
Sophie	Mauritanie
Félix	Mali
Thomas	Madagascar
Emma	
Hugo	

a   b   c   d   e

Cognates

There are a number of words which are the same (cognates) or similar (near cognates) in French and English. Be careful to notice any spelling differences and, for nouns, whether they are masculine or feminine. You can check this in a dictionary.

4 Qu'est-ce qu'il y a derrière chaque porte? Tu ouvres la porte? Écris 'oui' ou 'non' pour chaque lettre.

What's behind each door? Will you open the door? Write oui or non for each letter.

Exemple
non

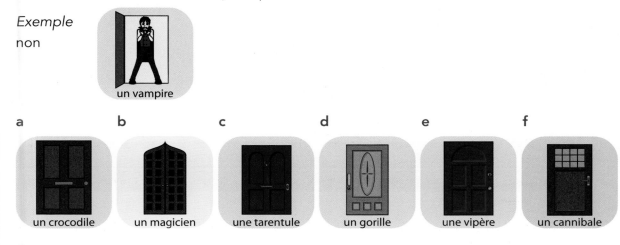

a	b	c	d	e	f
un crocodile	un magicien	une tarentule	un gorille	une vipère	un cannibale

5 Écris une liste de mots français qui sont pareils ou similaires en anglais.

Write a list of French words that you know which have the same or similar spelling in English and mean the same.

> une guitare (a guitar)
> intéressant (interesting)
> adorer (to love/to adore)

6 Identifie le verbe dans chaque phrase. Écris le mot que tu trouves dans le dictionnaire pour chaque verbe et la traduction en anglais.

Identify which word is the verb in each sentence. Look for each verb in the French section of the dictionary. Write down the word you find and its English translation. This word is called the infinitive.

1 Je joue avec mes copains.   2 On mange dans la cuisine.

3 Il regarde la télé dans le salon.   4 Elle déteste le théâtre.   5 Tu habites à Paris?

7 À deux, répondez aux questions.

In pairs, answer the questions.

1 What is a cognate?

2 Why is it useful to know if a French noun is masculine or feminine?

3 What form of a verb do you find in a dictionary?

4 What do you know now about using a dictionary that you didn't know before?

On fait du ski.

On joue au futsal.

On va au marché.

On nettoie l'aquarium.

On va aux marionettes.

Découverte du monde:

What do you and your friends and family do when you have some free time? What are your favourite activities and what do you not enjoy doing?

Le savais-tu?

Leisure activities are very important in France. Sport is particularly popular: over 30 million people take part in a sporting activity at least once a week. That's about half the population. Football and tennis are the most practised sports, but many others are very popular too. Handball, for example – the French national teams have been very successful in World Championships and the Olympic Games. Have you ever played handball?

1 Regarde la vidéo. Copie et complète le tableau en anglais. Écris un des symboles à côté de chaque activité.

Watch the video. Copy and complete the table. Write one of the symbols in the purple box next to each activity.

À la maison	À l'intérieur	À l'extérieur
	game with small ball ?	*skiing* ✗

✓ I've done this.

✗ I've never done this.

? What's this?

2 Ajoute au tableau des activités que tu fais ou d'autres activités que tu imagines qu'on va étudier. À deux, comparez vos listes.

Add to the table any activities you do or any other activities you think you might learn about in this module. In pairs, compare your lists.

Module 3: Ta mission...

- Talk about what more than one person does
- Use a wider range of regular and irregular verbs
- Talk about where my friends and I go at the weekend
- Use the verb *aller*
- Talk about a range of sports and activities

- Use *on peut* to talk about what you can do
- Describe family outings
- Talk about when and how often I do things
- Talk about my birthday
- Use *de* to express what belongs to someone
- Choose items from a menu using *prendre*
- Use *du, de la, de l'* and *des*

3 Topic 1 Le week-end chez moi

Objectifs
- Talk about what more than one person does
- Use a wider range of regular and irregular verbs

Langue et grammaire

Plural verbs

To talk about what more than one person does, use the plural form of a verb:

nous parlons	we speak/talk
vous parlez	you speak/talk
ils/elles parlent	they speak/talk

'They' can be *ils* or *elles*.
- Use *ils* to talk about
  - a group of people that includes at least one male
  - masculine plural nouns (or a group of masculine and feminine nouns)
- Use *elles* to talk about
  - a group of women
  - feminine plural nouns

More irregular verbs

You've met the irregular verbs *avoir* and *être*. In this topic, you'll be using the two irregular verbs below. Can you spot the irregularity?

faire	to do	**nettoyer**	to clean
je fais	nous faisons	je nettoie	nous nettoyons
tu fais	vous faites	tu nettoies	vous nettoyez
il/elle/on fait	ils/elles font	il/elle/on nettoie	ils/elles nettoient

Pronunciation

When you say *ils parlent* or *elles parlent*, you do not pronounce the –ent at the end. This means that *parle*, *parles* and *parlent* all sound the same.

---

1 Associe les phrases 1–6 avec les images a–f.
Match sentences 1–6 with the pictures a–f.

1 Je range ma chambre. **2** Je fais mes devoirs.

3 Je nettoie l'aquarium. **4** Je fais la vaisselle.

5 J'arrose les plantes. **6** Je fais les courses.

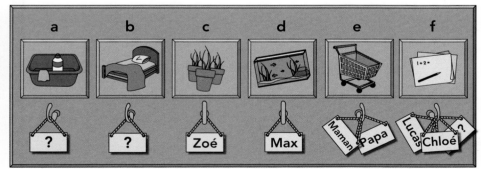

Vocabulaire

ranger	to tidy
nettoyer	to clean
arroser les plantes	to water the plants
louer un film	to rent a film
faire la vaisselle	to do the washing up
commander une pizza	to order a pizza
faire les courses	to do the shopping
se disputer	to argue
dîner	to have dinner
souvent	often
quelquefois	sometimes
normalement	usually
un aquarium	a fish tank
maman	mum
papa	dad

a Écoute et écris les noms et les lettres dans le bon ordre.
Listen and write the names and letters in the correct order.

b Écris les noms qui manquent pour les images a, b et f.
Write the names which are missing for pictures a, b and f.

3 Remplis les blancs avec les bons verbes.
Fill the gaps with the correct form of the verbs.

| range | fait | fais | font | fait | fait | arrose | nettoie |

Normalement, le weekend chez moi je **1** _____ mes devoirs et je **2** _____ ma chambre.
Mon frère **3** _____ l'aquarium et il **4** _____ aussi ses devoirs. Ma petite sœur **5** _____
les plantes et ma grande sœur **6** _____ la vaisselle et elle **7** _____ aussi ses devoirs. Mes
parents **8** _____ les courses.

4 À deux, regardez les informations de l'exercice 3. A pose des questions. B joue le rôle
de Lucas.
In pairs, look at the information in exercise 3. A asks questions. B plays the role of Lucas.

Qu'est-ce que tu fais?	Normalement, je...
Qu'est-ce que Chloé/Max/Zoé fait?	Chloé/Max/Zoé...
Qu'est-ce que tes parents font?	Mes parents...

5 'Toujours', 'souvent' ou 'quelquefois'? Écris la fréquence de chaque activité.
Always, often or sometimes? How often do Lucas's family do each thing?

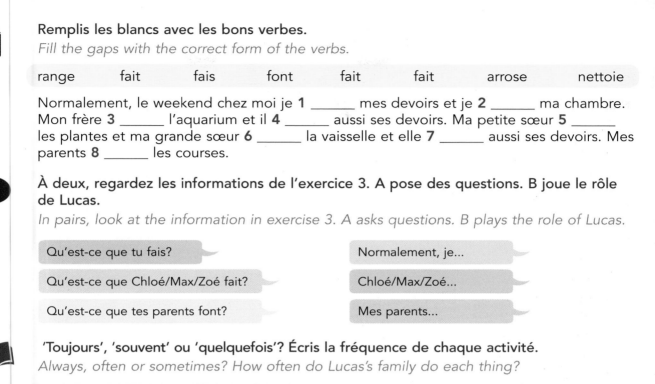

Hugo! Ça va, cousin?!

Merci pour ton e-mail. Le week-end? J'aime beaucoup le samedi soir. Nous dînons toujours à vingt heures et
souvent nous parlons de la semaine – c'est amusant parce que mon père est toujours très drôle. Quelquefois
nous commandons une pizza – j'adore les pizzas. Souvent mes parents louent un film – cool! Quelquefois nous
regardons le film ensemble dans le salon, mais ma petite sœur et mon frère se disputent toujours parce que
ma petite sœur est toujours à côté de maman et mon frère n'aime pas ça!

Et toi – tu aimes le week-end? Qu'est-ce que tu fais?

6 Utilise les phrases de l'exercice 5 pour traduire ces phrases. ⭐
*Use the sentences in exercise 5 to translate
these sentences.*

1 They always have dinner at eight o'clock.

2 They often talk about the week.

3 Sometimes they order a pizza.

4 Often we rent a film.

5 Sometimes they watch the film together.

6 We always argue.

Voie express

It is important to understand that verbs
vary according to their subject and that
while some follow regular patterns, others
do not and simply have to be learned.
Plural verb forms can be quite difficult to
learn. See if you can write out the plural
of *faire*, *regarder* and *parler* without
looking at your book.

Objectifs
- Talk about where my friends and I go at the weekend
- Use the verb *aller*

Langue et grammaire

The verb *aller* (to go)

Aller is another irregular verb. Look at how it is formed:

je vais	I go / am going
tu vas	you go / are going
il va	he goes / is going
elle va	she goes / is going
nous allons	we go / are going
vous allez	you go / are going
ils/elles vont	they go / are going

How to say 'to the'

Use *à la* when the place you are going to is feminine.
Use *au* when the place you are going to is masculine.
Use *aux* when the place you are going to is plural.
Use *à l'* when the place begins with a vowel or silent 'h'.

Elle va à la plage.	She's going to the beach.
Je vais au parc.	I'm going to the park.
Il va aux magasins.	He's going to the shops.
Nous allons à l'église.	We're going to the church.

 1 Lis et écoute. Écris le bon nom et le bon numéro. (1–7)
Read and listen. Write the correct name and the correct number.

Abdou   Emma   Félix   Justine   Maeva   Manon   Thomas

1 Je préfère aller au cinéma.

2 Je préfère aller à la plage.

3 Je préfère aller à la piscine.

4 Je préfère aller au centre d'équitation.

5 Je préfère aller au parc.

6 Je préfère aller au skate-parc.

7 Je préfère aller aux magasins.

2 Pose la question à 10 personnes. Fais un graphique de tes réponses, et complète la phrase: *L'activité la plus populaire est...*
Ask 10 people the question below. Show the answers in a bar or pie chart, and complete the sentence: L'activité la plus populaire est...

A Tu préfères aller où, ...?

B Je préfère aller au/à la/aux...

Vocabulaire

le skate-parc	the skate park
la piscine	the swimming pool
le centre d'équitation	the riding centre
les magasins	the shops
plus	more
préférer	to prefer
tranquille (m/f)	quiet
bruyant(e)	noisy
cher (m) / chère (f)	expensive
pas cher (m) / pas chère (f)	not expensive
gratuit(e)	free
passionnant(e)	exciting
je trouve que...	I find that...

3

a Écris 'au', 'à la' ou 'aux' pour chaque destination.
Write au, à la or aux for each destination.

1 Je vais _____ centre d'équitation.

2 Nous allons _____ plage.

3 Tu vas _____ skate-parc?

4 Maeva va _____ piscine.

5 Mes parents vont _____ magasins.

6 Vous allez _____ parc?

7 Il va _____ cinéma.

b Écoute et vérifie tes réponses.
Listen and check your answers.

c Traduis les phrases en anglais.
Translate the sentences into English.

4

Écoute et choisis la bonne raison pour chaque personne.
Listen and choose the correct reason for each person.

a Manon ~~cool~~/génial

b Emma intéressant/amusant

c Abdou passionnant/pas cher

d Maeva génial/cool

e Justine super/amusant

f Félix amusant/intéressant

g Thomas super/pas cher

Voie express

There is a lot of useful learning here. You will often use the verb *aller*, but it is very irregular! You need to learn all forms by heart and use it accurately. The vocabulary will help you talk about the things that interest you. Write a family journal for a weekend, describing what everyone does.

5

Parlez à deux. A pose les questions. B répond. Puis changez de rôles.
Work in pairs. A asks the questions and B replies. Then swap roles.

A Tu préfères aller où?

B Je préfère aller au/à la/aux...

A Pourquoi?

B Parce que c'est cool/ce n'est pas cher...

6

Lis et remplis les blancs avec les parties du verbe 'aller'.
Read and fill the gaps in the text with the correct form of aller.
Then fill the gaps in the English sentences.

Félix va toujours au cinéma mais moi, je ne veux pas. Je **1**_____ au skate-parc parce que c'est passionnant et bruyant. Et toi, Thomas, tu **2** _____ où?

Manon et sa copine, elles **3**_____ au centre d'équitation, mais je n'aime pas ça. Mon copain et moi, nous **4** _____ au parc, parce que c'est tranquille et c'est gratuit!

a Abdou prefers going to the _____ because he thinks it's _____.

b Thomas prefers going to the _____ because he thinks it's _____.

3 Topic 3 Un week-end actif

Objectifs
- Talk about a range of sports and activities
- Use *on peut* with *faire* or *jouer* to talk about what you can do

Langue et grammaire

Talking about sport

Use *faire* (to do) or *jouer* (to play) to talk about doing different sports.

For sports that are masculine use *faire du* or *jouer au*:
Je fais du roller.
Je joue au basket.

For sports that are feminine use *faire de la* or *jouer à la*:

Je fais de la danse.
Je joue à la pétanque.

Remember, if the sport begins with a vowel use *l'*:
Je fais de l'escrime.

Talking about what you can do

Use *on peut* with *faire* or *jouer* to talk about what you **can** do.

Au centre sportif on peut jouer au tennis. — At the sports centre you can play tennis.
On peut faire de la boxe. — You can do boxing.

1 a Regarde le programme et choisis les bons mots pour chaque sport.

Look at the timetable and choose the correct words for each sport.

> jouer à la   jouer au   faire de la
> faire du   faire de l'

b Écoute et vérifie tes réponses.

Listen and check your answers.

Centre Sportif Charles Moureu

| Qui sommes-nous? | Les news | Programme | Visite |

Centre Sportif Charles Moureu – Programme du week-end

samedi matin
a handball
b tennis
c danse

samedi après-midi
d roller & skate
e escrime

dimanche matin
f basket
g boxe
h futsal

dimanche après-midi
i pétanque

2 Regardez les programmes et parlez à deux.

Look at the timetables and speak in pairs.

Exemple

A Qu'est-ce qu'on peut faire samedi matin au Centre Sportif Bouger?

B Samedi matin au Centre Sportif Bouger on peut...

Vocabulaire

le roller	roller-blading
le skate	skateboarding
la boxe	boxing
l'escrime (f)	fencing
le handball	handball
le futsal	futsal (indoor five-a-side football)
le basket	basketball
la danse	dance
la pétanque	boules (a French version of bowls)
le tennis	tennis
violent(e)	violent
la natation	swimming
la gymnastique	gymnastics
le rugby	rugby
la plongée	diving
l'athlétisme	athletics

3 Écris deux phrases pour expliquer ce qu'on peut faire aux centres sportifs.
Write two sentences about what you can do at the sports centres.

Voie express

You need to be clear about the difference between *jouer* and *faire*. A lot of sports and activities sound very similar in French and English, so these words are quick to learn. Cover the English words in the *Vocabulaire* – how many of the French words can you translate without even trying to learn them? Now cover the French words – how many can you translate the other way?

4 a Lis les bulles. Vrai ou faux?
Read the speech bubbles. True or false?

Le samedi matin je vais au Centre Sportif Moureu avec ma sœur. Je fais du roller et ma sœur fait de la danse. Je préfère le roller parce que je pense que c'est passionnant et ce n'est pas tranquille!

Le dimanche matin je vais au Centre Sportif Moureu avec mon frère. Je joue au futsal et mon frère fait de la boxe. Je préfère le futsal parce que je pense que c'est amusant et ce n'est pas violent!

Le samedi après-midi je vais au stade avec mon frère. Je joue au rugby, et mon frère fait de l'athlétisme et de la gymnastique. Je préfère le rugby parce que c'est bruyant, et la gymnastique n'est pas facile.

Le samedi matin je vais à la piscine avec ma copine. Je fais de la natation et elle fait de la plongée. Je préfère la natation parce que c'est amusant et ce n'est pas difficile.

1 Lucas goes to the sports centre on Saturdays.

2 Justine goes to the sports centre with her sister.

3 Justine's sister does fencing.

4 Lucas plays futsal.

5 Abdou does athletics.

6 Manon goes to the swimming pool with her friend.

b Lis et réponds aux questions en anglais.
Read and answer the questions in English.

1 What sport does Justine do?

2 What sport does Lucas's brother do?

3 Why does Justine prefer roller-blading?

4 Why does Lucas prefer futsal?

5 Why does Abdou prefer rugby?

6 Why does Manon prefer swimming?

5 Écris un paragraphe pour décrire les sports que tu fais le week-end avec un(e) ami(e).
Write a paragraph to describe a sporting day with a friend.

6 Donnez des présentations de l'exercice 5 en petits groupes.
Give presentations of your work from exercise 5 in small groups.

Objectifs
- Describe family outings
- Talk about when and how often I do things

Langue et grammaire

Nous allons, nous faisons

Remember that *nous* is always followed by a verb ending in *–ons*:

nous regardons	we watch
nous jouons	we play

The verb *aller* follows the same pattern:

nous allons	we go

Note that the *nous* form of the verb *faire* has an 's':

nous faisons	we do

Talking about the seasons

The word *en* is used to talk about a season, except for spring when you use *au* instead:

en été	in summer
en automne	in autumn
en hiver	in winter
au printemps	in spring

1 **Sépare les mots pour trouver une phrase pour chaque image.**
Separate the words to find a phrase for each picture.

a b c d

nousfaisonsunebaladeàlacampagnenousfaisonsunbarbecuenousfaisonsduskinousfaisonsduvélo

2 **Mets les lettres des mots soulignés dans le bon ordre pour trouver les saisons. Réponds aux questions en anglais.**
Unscramble the underlined words to find the seasons. Answer the questions in English.

1 De temps en temps en **etanmuo** nous faisons du vélo.

2 Une fois par semaine en **téé** nous faisons un barbecue.

3 De temps en temps au **rtpispmen** nous faisons une balade à la campagne.

4 Une fois par mois, en **rvhie** nous faisons du ski.

A What do they do in summer?   B What do they do in winter?

C What do they do in spring?   D What do they do in autumn?

3 **Écoute et complète les phrases.**
Listen and complete the sentences.

a Sophie fait _____ de temps en temps en _____.

b Justine fait un barbecue _____ en _____.

c Félix fait _____ de _____ au printemps.

d Hugo fait du ski une _____ en _____.

Voie express

You are learning a lot of new vocabulary and expanding the range of things you can talk about. Using some of the new expressions in your work will make it more interesting and more fluent. List all the leisure activities you know in French and write down how often and when you usually do each one.

4 Remplis les blancs avec des mots de la boîte.
Fill the gaps with the words from the box.

faisons	année	balade	automne
ski	printemps	allons	fois

1 De temps en temps, en _____, nous _____ du vélo.

2 Une _____ par semaine, en été, nous _____ à la plage.

3 Chaque _____, en hiver, nous faisons du _____.

4 Une fois par mois, au _____, nous faisons une _____ à la campagne.

Vocabulaire

faire du ski	to go skiing
faire du vélo	to go cycling
faire une balade	to go for a walk
à la campagne	in the countryside
un barbecue	a barbecue
une sortie	an outing
une exposition	an exhibition
les marionnettes	a puppet show
un spectacle	sound and
son et lumière	light show
une image	a picture
de temps	occasionally, from
en temps	time to time
une fois par mois	once a month
chaque année	every year
une place	a town square

5 Parlez à deux.
Speak in pairs.

A Tu fais des sorties en famille quelquefois?

B

Oui	de temps en temps	en hiver	nous...
	une fois/deux fois par semaine	au printemps	
	une fois/deux fois par mois	en été	
		en automne	

6 Lis, copie et complète le tableau. ⭐
Read, copy and complete the table.

often	sometimes	occasionally	every year
theatre is	they go to	theatre is	go to aunt's
interesting	the theatre	funny	house

Ma tante habite à Nancy. Chaque année, en été, on va chez elle et on fait une grande sortie en famille – il y a ma sœur et moi, mes deux cousins, ma mère et mon père, et mon oncle et ma tante. Quelquefois on va au théâtre. J'aime beaucoup le théâtre – je pense que souvent c'est très intéressant et de temps en temps c'est drôle aussi. Quelquefois on va à une exposition – de temps en temps c'est passionnant mais souvent je trouve que c'est un peu ennuyeux. Souvent on va au spectacle son et lumière sur la place Stanislas au centre ville. J'adore ça – on écoute la musique et on regarde les lumières et les images – c'est génial! Ma sœur n'aime pas le spectacle son et lumière parce que c'est le soir et elle est fatiguée. Elle préfère aller aux marionnettes dans le parc de la Pépinière parce qu'elle pense que c'est plus amusant.

7 Écris un paragraphe pour décrire les sorties que tu fais avec ta famille ou tes amis. ⭐
Write a paragraph about the outings you go on with your family or friends.

Objectifs
- Talk about my birthday
- Use *de* to express what belongs to someone

Langue et grammaire

Talking about what belongs to someone

In English, you use the letter 's' to talk about what belongs to someone. For example, 'Marie's brother'. In French, use *de* (or *d'* before a vowel) like this:

le frère de Marie   la guitare d'Abdou   l'anniversaire de Sophie

Months and dates

Like the days of the week, the months of the year are written without a capital letter in French.

To say that your birthday is in a particular month use *en* before the month:

Mon anniversaire est en mai.   My birthday is in May.

To say that your birthday is on a particular date use *le* before the date:

Mon anniversaire est le quinze mai.   My birthday is on 15 May.

Abbreviations

It is very common in French for long words to be shortened by dropping one or more syllables at the end. The word *anniversaire* is a good example – sometimes it's shortened to just *anniv*.

Boire

The verb *boire* (to drink) is another important irregular verb:

je bois	I drink
tu bois	you drink
il/elle boit	he/she drinks
on boit	we drink

---

1 Écris une phrase pour chaque personne dans le carnet.

Write a sentence for each person in the book.

Exemple   L'anniversaire de Manon est en avril.

2 a Écoute et vérifie tes réponses.

Listen and check your answers.

b Écoute et associe les noms et les dates.

Listen and match the names and the dates.

1 Sophie	**2** Félix	**3** Emma	**4** Marie	**5** Hugo	**6** Dan
a 10/02	**b** 30/11	**c** 01/10	**d** 07/01	**e** 11/07	**f** 16/06

3 Fais un sondage de 12 personnes.
Do a survey of 12 people.

A C'est quand ton anniversaire?

B Mon anniversaire est le 26 mars.

4 Fais un graphique des résultats du sondage de l'exercice 3. Les anniversaires sont en quels mois?

Make a graph of the results of the survey in exercise 3. Which months are the birthdays in?

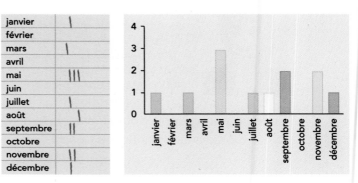

Vocabulaire

un anniv(ersaire)	a birthday
une fête	a party
janvier	January
février	February
mars	March
avril	April
mai	May
juin	June
juillet	July
août	August
septembre	September
octobre	October
novembre	November
décembre	December
une soirée pyjama	a pyjama party
d'abord	first
ensuite	then/next
après	after
finalement	finally
danser	to dance
un gâteau d'anniversaire	a birthday cake

5 Écoute et écris 'Manon' ou 'Félix' pour chaque phrase.
Listen and write Manon or Félix for each sentence.

1 _____ 's birthday is on 16 June.

2 _____ 's birthday is on 25 April.

3 _____ has a pyjama party.

4 _____ invites some friends to go bowling.

5 _____ likes it a lot because it's brilliant.

6 _____ loves it because it's lots of fun.

6 a Écris les lettres dans le bon ordre.
Write the letters in the correct order.

À la soirée pyjama

D'abord, on écoute de la musique et on chante ou on danse.

Ensuite, on mange des pizzas et on boit du cola ou du jus de fruit.

Après, il y a le gâteau d'anniversaire.

Et finalement, on va au lit!

a  b  c  d

b Lis et compare la fête au bowling avec la soirée pyjama. Écris deux listes en anglais.
Read and compare the bowling party with the pyjama party. Write two lists in English.

À la fête au bowling

D'abord, on joue au bowling.

Ensuite on mange des hot-dogs et on boit du cola ou du jus de fruit.

Après il y a du gâteau d'anniversaire.

Finalement on rentre chez nous.

Voie express

Test yourself! See if you can write the 12 months of the year in French correctly without looking at the *Vocabulaire* box. Imagine what type of party another person in your class usually has and write a panel about it like the ones in exercises 6 and 7.

7 Décris une fête d'anniversaire pour ton blog au Forum des francophones.
Describe a birthday party for your blog on the Forum des francophones.

Objectifs
- Choose items from a menu
- Use more irregular verbs

Langue et grammaire

Choosing from a menu

To say what you'd like to eat, use the verb *prendre* (to take). *Prendre* is an irregular verb. Look at how it works:

je prends	I take
tu prends	you take
il/elle prend	he/she takes

Here are some examples:

Qu'est-ce que tu prends?	What are you having?
Je prends une pizza.	I'm having a pizza.

How to say 'some'

The word for 'some' in French depends upon whether the noun you're talking about is masculine, feminine or plural, or begins with a vowel:

du cola	some cola
du jus de fruit	some fruit juice
de la limonade	some lemonade
de l'eau	some water
des champignons	some mushrooms
des tomates	some tomatoes

 1 Écoute et associe les plats avec les restaurants.

Listen and match the dishes with the restaurants.

1  **2**  **3**  **4** Hang Ho

a  **b**  **c**  **d**

une pizza   des nouilles   une galette   un tajine

2 Écoute encore. Vrai ou faux?
Listen again. True or false?

1 It's Sophie's dad's birthday.

2 Sophie loves pizza.

3 Sophie's mum loves pizza too.

4 Hang Ho is a Moroccan restaurant.

5 Sophie hates noodles.

6 Sophie would really like to go to Le Timgad.

7 Sophie says her mum loves galettes and crêpes.

8 They decide to go to Chez Melec.

Voie express

You may already know some of the food items in the vocabulary here and you may know others that are not listed. Be sure to learn all the new items and make sure you can use *prendre* correctly. When you can do that, you could create your own menu and invent names for the different dishes. Think of food items that use French names in English such as *croissant*, *pain au chocolat* and *baguette*.

Vocabulaire

marocain(e)	Moroccan
vietnamien(ne)	Vietnamese
une crêperie	creperie/pancake restaurant
une crêpe	a sweet pancake
une galette	a savoury pancake
un tajine	a tagine
les nouilles	noodles
le fromage	cheese
l'eau (f)	water
un œuf	an egg
le jambon	ham
les champignons	mushrooms
les pommes	apples
la tomate	tomato
l'oignon (m)	onion
sucré	sweet
salé	savoury
le beurre	butter
le sucre	sugar
le chocolat	chocolate
le menu à 12,50€	the 12.50€ menu
la limonade	lemonade

3 Lis le menu et la conversation. Est-ce que Sophie fait des bons choix? Réponds en anglais.

Read the menu. Listen to Sophie. Does she make the right choices? Reply in English.

Le menu 12,50€
Les salées

La complète
fromage – jambon – œuf

La forestière
œuf – jambon – champignons

La végétarienne
champignons – tomates – oignons

Le menu 12,50€
Les sucrées

La simple
beurre – sucre

La parisienne
chocolat

La normande
pommes

Qu'est-ce que tu prends, Sophie?

Je ne prends pas La végétarienne parce que je déteste les oignons. J'adore le fromage donc je prends La complète. Et en sucré – je n'aime pas le beurre et je n'aime pas les pommes, mais j'adore le chocolat donc je prends La normande.

4 a Relis le menu et regarde les informations. Choisis un menu pour la mère et le père de Sophie. ⭐

Read the menu again, look at the information. Choose a menu for Sophie's mum and dad.

b Écris une réponse pour la mère et le père de Sophie. Pourquoi font-ils ces choix?

Write an answer for Sophie's mum and dad. Why do they make these choices?

	❤ aime/adore	✖ n'aime pas/déteste
Maman		
Papa		

5 Parlez à deux.

Speak in pairs.

A Qu'est-ce que tu prends _____?

B Je n'aime pas _____, mais j'adore _____, donc je prends _____. Et en sucrée _____.

6 Écoute la conversation. Qu'est-ce qu'ils choisissent?

Listen to the conversation. What do they choose to drink?

Langue et grammaire

Plural verbs

There are two French words for 'you'.
Use *tu* to talk to one person you know well.
Use *vous* to talk to more than one person, or to someone you don't know very well.

There are also two French words for 'they'.
Use *ils* to talk about
- a group of people that includes at least one male
- masculine plural nouns (or a group of masculine and feminine nouns)

Use *elles* to talk about
- a group of women
- feminine plural nouns

Nous

Nous is always followed by a verb ending in –ons:

nous regardons	we watch
nous jouons	we play
nous allons	we go
nous faisons	we do

The verb *aller* (to go)

Aller (to go) is a very important irregular verb:

je vais	I go / am going
tu vas	you go / are going
il/elle va	he/she goes / is going
on va	we go / are going (informal)
nous allons	we go / are going
vous allez	you go / are going
ils/elles vont	they go / are going

Saying what you'd like to eat and drink

The verb *boire* (to drink) is an irregular verb:

je bois	I drink	tu bois	you drink
il/elle/on boit		he/she/we drink(s)	

To say what you'd like to eat, use the verb *prendre* (to take), another irregular verb:

je prends	I take	tu prends	you take
il/elle/on prend		he/she/we take(s)	

How to say 'to the'

Use *au* for masculine places: *au cinéma*.
Use *à la* for feminine places: *à la plage*.

Use *aux* for places which are plural: *aux magasins*.
Use *à l'* if the place begins with a vowel or silent 'h': *à l'exposition*.

How to say 'some'

Use *du* for masculine nouns: *du jambon*.
Use *de la* for feminine nouns: *de la limonade*.
Use *des* for plural nouns: *des pommes*.
Use *de l'* for nouns beginning with a vowel or silent 'h': *de l'eau*.

Talking about sports

Use *faire du* or *jouer au* for masculine sports.
Use *faire de la* or *jouer à la* for feminine sports.
Use *faire de l'* or *jouer à l'* if the sport begins with a vowel.

Je fais du roller.	Je fais de la danse.
Je fais de l'escrime.	

Saying what you are able to do

Use *on peut* with *faire* or *jouer* to say what you can do:
Au parc on peut jouer au tennis.

Months and dates

To say the month of your birthday, use *en* before the month:

Mon anniversaire est en mai.	My birthday is in May.

To say the date of your birthday, use *le* before the date:

Mon anniversaire est le 15 mai.	My birthday is on 15 May.

Seasons

Use *en* to talk about a season, except for spring when you use *au*:

en été	in summer	en automne	in autumn
en hiver	in winter	au printemps	in spring

Talking about what belongs to someone

Use *de* (or *d'* before a vowel):

le frère de Marie	Marie's brother
la guitare d'Abdou	Abdou's guitar

Vocabulaire

Les activités
arroser les plantes
nettoyer l'aquarium
ranger sa chambre
louer un film
faire la vaisselle
faire les courses
commander une pizza
se disputer
dîner
danser
une soirée pyjama
un barbecue

Les sports
la natation
la gymnastique
le rugby
la plongée
l'athlétisme (m)
faire du ski
faire du vélo
faire une balade
à la campagne

Les endroits
le cinéma
le skate-parc
la plage
la piscine
le centre d'équitation
les magasins
la fête
la sortie
le spectacle
la place
la crêperie
l'exposition (f)
les marionnettes (f)

Les mots de fréquence
après
d'abord
ensuite
finalement
de temps en temps
une fois/deux fois par
  mois
chaque année
souvent
quelquefois
normalement

Les dates
janvier
février
mars
avril
mai
juin
juillet
août
septembre
octobre
novembre
décembre
un anniv(ersaire)

Les mots utiles
je trouve que…
plus
préférer

La nourriture
la crêpe
la galette
le tajine
les nouilles (f)
le fromage
le pain
l'œuf (m)

le jambon
les champignons (m)
les pommes (f)
la tomate
le gâteau
le beurre
le sucre
le chocolat
l'oignon (m)
la limonade
l'eau (f)
le menu à 12,50€
sucré
salé

Les adjectifs
tranquille
bruyant(e)
(pas) cher (m) /
  (pas) chère (f)
gratuit(e)
passionnant(e)
marocain(e)
vietnamien(ne)
violent(e)

Mission accomplie?

I can...

- Talk about what more than one person does
- Use a wider range of regular and irregular verbs
- Talk about where my friends and I go at the weekend
- Use the verb *aller*
- Talk about a range of sports and activities
- Use *on peut* to talk about what you can do
- Describe family outings
- Talk about when and how often I do things
- Talk about my birthday
- Use *de* to express what belongs to someone
- Choose items from a menu using *prendre*
- Use *du, de la, de l'* and *des*

1

a Écris la liste de verbes français par ordre alphabétique et écris la traduction en anglais.
Write the list of French verbs in alphabetical order and write the English meanings.

danser	écouter	aller	chanter	jouer
parler	regarder	préférer	manger	inviter

b Associe ces verbes français avec les traductions en anglais.
Match these French verbs with their English translations.

1 arroser   **2** boire   **3** commander   **4** faire

5 louer   **6** nettoyer   **7** prendre   **8** ranger

9 rentrer   **10** se disputer

a to clean   **b** to tidy   **c** to go home   **d** to argue

e to water   **f** to order   **g** to drink   **h** to rent

i to do   **j** to take

elle jou–   nous jou–   il jou–   on jou–   **jouer**   tu jou–   je jou–   vous jou–   ils jou–   elles jou–

–e   –es   –ons   –ez   –ent

2 Copie l'image et choisis la bonne terminaison pour chaque partie du verbe.
Copy the picture and choose the correct ending for each part of the verb.

3 Crée d'autres images pour d'autres verbes de l'exercice 1.
Make more verb pictures with other verbs from exercise 1.

4 Regarde les images et complète les phrases.
Look at the pictures and complete the sentences.

Exemple **1** Je vais au centre d'équitation.

vais	au	plage
vas	à la	piscine
va	aux	centre d'équitation
allons		parc
allez		cinéma
vont		skate-parc
		magasins

1
De temps en temps je _____.

2
Une fois par semaine elle_____.

3
Quelquefois nous _____.

4
Deux fois par mois ils _____.

5
Chaque année on _____.

6
Tu _____?

7
Vous _____?

5 Traduis les phrases de l'exercice 4.
Translate the sentences from exercise 4.

Exemple **1** From time to time I go to the riding centre.

6 Tu as une bonne mémoire? C'est qui? Utilise les mots de la liste.
Do you have a good memory? Who is it? Use the words from the list.

la petite sœur	la correspondante	la mère	le cousin
le petit frère	le correspondant	la grande sœur	

1 2 3 4 5 6 7

Exemple **1** Elle est la petite sœur de Lucas. Elle s'appelle Zoé.

7 **a** Remplis les blancs avec les bons mots.
Fill the gaps with correct phrase.

joue au   joue à la   fait du   fait de la

Max **1** _____ danse et Lucie **2** _____ boxe. Lucas **3** _____ handball et Justine **4** _____ roller.

En hiver, Hugo **5** _____ ski une fois par mois et en automne Sophie **6** _____ skate de temps

en temps. Le père de Félix **7** _____ pétanque au centre sportif le dimanche après-midi.

b Note les numéros des images qui ne correspondent pas aux informations.
Note the numbers of the pictures which don't fit the written information.

1 2 3 4

5 6 7

c Écris le paragraphe avec les bonnes informations.
Write the paragraph with the correct information.

Le blog Découverte

S'IDENTIFIER
inscrire

FORUMS   MEMBRES   BLOGS   GALERIE

Quels sont tes jeux préférés?
Tu joues à quoi quand tu es chez toi avec tes copains, avec ta famille ou tout(e) seul(e)? Quels jeux préfères-tu et pourquoi?

posté par Maeva, 12 ans
Avec mes cousins je joue souvent à la DS, avec mes copains je joue sur la Wii et quand je suis toute <u>seule</u> je joue sur l'ordinateur ou, de temps en temps, sur l'iPad de ma mère. J'aime <u>l'ordinateur</u> mais, pour moi, l'iPad est plus intéressant parce qu'on peut faire beaucoup de choses différentes.

posté par Lucas, 12 ans
Moi, je joue sur la Wii ou sur la PS3 avec mon frère. Nous jouons ensemble tous les week-ends quand nous avons du temps libre. Je joue sur l'ordi aussi – c'est super parce que, avec mon cousin, Hugo (qui habite au Canada), on peut jouer en ligne. Je n'aime pas beaucoup les jeux de société mais de temps en temps je joue aux cartes avec mes copains.

posté par Justine, 12 ans
J'adore les jeux vidéo et quelquefois sur l'ordi je joue au Tetris. Je joue beaucoup aux jeux sur mon portable – c'est très pratique. En <u>jeu de société</u> je joue au Scrabble ou au Trivial Poursuite. En fait, les jeux de société sont plus amusants quand on est avec beaucoup de copains parce que tout le monde peut jouer.

posté par Abdou, 12 ans
Je ne joue jamais avec des <u>jouets</u> – pas maintenant. Je préfère les jeux vidéo et je joue souvent sur la Wii ou, quand je suis tout seul ou très fatigué le soir, je joue sur la tablette de mon père. C'est cool! Je ne joue pas souvent aux jeux de société – je trouve ça un peu ennuyeux.

posté par Sophie, 12 ans
Moi, quand je suis toute seule, je joue sur la tablette. Quelquefois, avec ma petite sœur, je joue avec des jouets – elle adore le Playmobil. Quand je suis avec mes copains on joue sur la Wii. Mais quand je suis en famille je joue au Cluedo ou au Monopoly – nous jouons souvent le dimanche après-midi. Moi, je pense que les jeux de société sont très amusants.

1 **a Lis le texte. Cherche les mots soulignés dans le dictionnaire.**
Read the text. Look up the underlined words in a dictionary.

b Vrai ou faux?
True or false?

1 Maeva plays on her mum's iPad.   **2** Justine plays Trivial Pursuit or Monopoly.

3 Sophie loves Playmobil.   **4** Lucas plays on the Wii with his brother.

5 Abdou likes board games a lot.

2 **Qui...**
Who...

a ... plays on a tablet?   **b** ... plays on the Wii with friends?

c ... thinks board games are fun?   **d** ... doesn't like board games much?

e ... never plays with toys?

3 Réponds aux questions en anglais.
Answer the questions in English.

a What does Lucas sometimes do with his friends?

b What does Sophie sometimes do with her little sister?

c What does Justine love?

d What does Sophie's sister love?

e Who does Maeva play on the DS with?

4 Trouve tous les mots qu'on utilise pour parler de quand et combien de fois on fait quelque chose. Écris et traduis ces mots.
Find all the time and frequency expressions in the text. These are the words and expressions we use to say when or how often we do something. Write and translate them.

5 Utilise les mots de l'exercice 4 pour écrire des phrases sur toi en français.
Use the words and expressions from exercise 4 to write some sentences about yourself.

6 Trouve le français pour ces mots dans le texte.
Find the French for these phrases in the text.

a when I'm with my family

b when I'm on my own

c when I'm with my friends

d with my cousins

e with my brother

f with my little sister

g everyone

7 Traduis la réponse au blog Découverte de Dan. Utilise un dictionnaire s'il y a un mot difficile.
Translate Dan's reply to the Découverte blog. Use a dictionary for difficult or unfamiliar words.

S'IDENTIFIER
inscrire

Le blog **Découverte**

FORUMS   MEMBRES   BLOGS   GALERIE

Dan, 12 ans
I'm always playing games on my mobile – it's relaxing when I'm tired. When I'm with my friends I love playing on the Wii – we play together when we have free time – I think it's fun! Sometimes I play on my brother's tablet. I love that because you can play on your own or online with your friends. I often play with my cousins in France – it's cool! I never play board games – they are a lot less interesting.

8 Poste une réponse sur toi sur le blog Découverte.
Post a reply about yourself on the blog Découverte.

Un anniversaire et un accident

Read the latest episode of the bande dessinée *using the pictures to help you. Check your understanding by discussing the story in pairs.*

1 JUSTINE, QUE FAIT TA SŒUR LUCIE LE WEEK-END?

AH, DONC TU AIMES VRAIMENT LUCIE! MA SŒUR AIME BEAUCOUP LA MUSIQUE ET ELLE EST TRÈS SPORTIVE. LE WEEK-END ELLE FAIT DE LA DANSE ET ELLE JOUE AU BASKET — ELLE ADORE ÇA!

2 OH, C'EST LA FÊTE POUR MON ANNIV SAMEDI APRÈS-MIDI. MA SŒUR VA...

SUPER!

C'EST MA CHANCE!

3 ÉCOUTEZ! M. VILAIN A L'IDÉE DE TRANSFORMER LE PARC EN PARKING!

CE N'EST PAS POSSIBLE! TOUT LE MONDE ADORE LE PARC!

C'EST VRAI! NOUS ALLONS AU PARC TOUS LES WEEK-ENDS ET EN ÉTÉ NOUS FAISONS DES BARBECUES. J'ADORE ÇA!

ET LE FESTIVAL DE MUSIQUE?!

4 MAIS ON PEUT SAUVER LE PARC! M. VILAIN A UN RENDEZ-VOUS SAMEDI SOIR, ET NOUS Y ALLONS AUSSI!

5 C'EST SAMEDI, LE JOUR DE LA FÊTE POUR L'ANNIVERSAIRE DE JUSTINE.

Résumé

C'est le week-end et Abdou et Justine vont au parc. Ils parlent de la sœur de Justine, parce qu'Abdou l'aime beaucoup. Elle s'appelle Lucie et elle est très sportive. Le week-end, elle préfère jouer au basket et faire de la natation. Elle adore la musique, donc elle fait de la danse aussi. Il y a une fête samedi après-midi pour l'anniversaire de Justine. Abdou va à la fête et Lucie y va aussi. C'est l'occasion idéale pour parler avec elle!

Quand ils trouvent les autres amis, Lucas parle de l'idée de M. Vilain de transformer le parc en parking. C'est une idée horrible! Ils vont au parc très souvent: on peut faire du vélo, on peut jouer au tennis et on peut faire des barbecues. Et il est très beau aussi! Mais Lucas a une idée. Samedi soir, Monsieur Vilain a un rendez-vous avec Monsieur Dupont. Les amis vont écouter la conversation.

Samedi arrive. La fête est très amusante. Les amis écoutent de la musique, dansent et mangent de la nourriture délicieuse. Il y a de la pizza, des hot-dogs, du fromage et du pain. Il y a aussi le gâteau au chocolat bien sûr! Abdou apporte de la limonade à Lucie, mais il tombe et il renverse la limonade sur sa robe: quel désastre! Il est vraiment désolé.

Il est 18h30, l'heure de partir. On y va!

Activité

In groups, choose a scene to perform. You could use a scene from this comic strip or from the one you produced in Module 2. Think about your tone of voice – try to be expressive!

Gender

In French, nouns are either masculine or feminine – this is known as the gender of a noun. It's easy to know the gender of a noun if it refers to a person. However, in French all nouns have a gender, not just nouns used to talk about people. It's important to know the gender of a noun so that:

- Your French is accurate.
- You can decide which form of other words, for example adjectives, to use with it.
- You do not mix up words which are spelled the same but have both a masculine and a feminine form with two very different meanings. For example, *le vase* means the same as the English word 'vase', but *la vase* means 'mud'!

 1 À deux. Sans regarder dans le dictionnaire, devinez le genre de ces mots. Masculin ou féminin (*un* ou *une*)?

In pairs. Without looking in a dictionary, guess the gender of these words. Masculine or feminine (un or une)? What do you notice about the endings of the words and how does that help you to decide?

> acteur   actrice   princesse   prince
> boulanger   boulangère   électricienne   électricien

 2 Écris une liste d'autres noms pour les personnes.
Write a list of as many nouns for people as you can. Include the article un *or* une.

 3 *Look in the dictionary to find out the gender of these words. Write each word in the correct category in the table. When you have finished, what do you notice about the endings of the words in each category?*

orage   vêtement   liberté   poignée   sondage   potage   beauté   fumée   monument   santé

masculine	feminine

4 **a** *Consider your answers in exercise 3. Here is one list of feminine endings and one list of masculine endings. Choose the correct title for each list of word endings.*

b Sans regarder dans le dictionnaire – ces mots sont de quel genre?
Without checking in a dictionary, decide if these words are masculine or feminine.

1 plombier
2 téléphone
3 impression
4 différence
5 pantalon
6 lecture
7 parachutisme
8 favorite

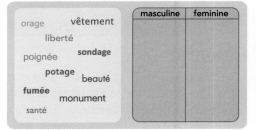

feminine endings	masculine endings
A	**B**
–ment	–sion
–eur	–ure
–oir	–té
–age	–euse
–ier	–ite
–on	–ée
–isme	–esse
–phone	–ence

5 Utilise le dictionnaire pour traduire ces mots et puis cherche le sens du mot de l'autre genre.

Use a dictionary to translate these words then find out what the word means when it has the opposite gender.

Exemple **a** a book *un livre (m)* *une livre (f)* = pound (weight)

b a sail _____ _____

c a sleeve _____ _____

d fashion _____ _____

e the post office _____ _____

Gender and adjectives

Remember, adjectives are spelled differently depending on the gender of the word they are describing. Use your dictionary to check the gender of the word you want to describe so that you can decide which form of the adjective to use.

When you look up an adjective in a dictionary you will first find the spelling used for describing a masculine word – the masculine form of the adjective.

For example, when you look in a dictionary for the word 'interesting', you will find the masculine form of the adjective *intéressant*. You can only use this with a noun that is masculine:

un film intéressant an interesting film

As you know already, for many adjectives, to create the feminine form of the adjective you simply need to add an 'e':

une histoire intéressante an interesting story

> But be careful – not all adjectives follow this pattern! For example, you've already come across the adjective *cher,* which becomes *chère* when describing a feminine noun.

6 *Use what you know about word endings or your dictionary to find out the gender of these words. Write* un *or* une. *Choose the correct form of the adjective and translate each phrase.*

Exemple **1** un oiseau bleu (a blue bird)

1 oiseau	bleu/bleue	
3 téléphone	noir/noire	
5 boisson	chaud/chaude	
7 dinosaure	vert/verte	

2 conversation	intéressant/intéressante	
4 robe	élégant/élégante	
6 matin	ensoleillé/ensoleillée	
8 poème	amusant/amusante	

4 Escapades

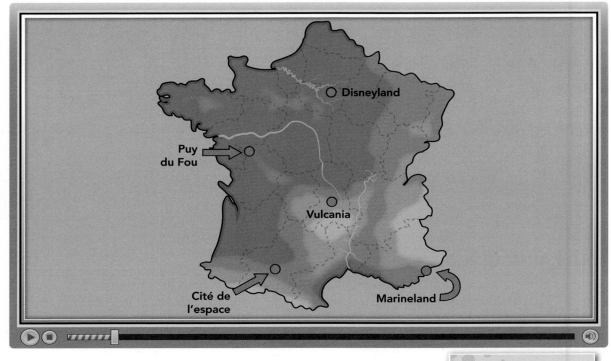

Disneyland

Puy du Fou

Vulcania

Cité de l'espace

Marineland

Les parcs d'attractions

Le parc de Vulcania, dans le centre de la France.

Le parc du Puy du Fou, dans l'ouest de la France.

Le parc de la Cité de l'espace, dans le sud-ouest de la France.

Le parc de Marineland, dans le sud-est de la France.

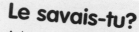

Découverte du monde:

Some adventure parks are based around fictional characters such as Astérix; others are a fun way of learning more about science or history or other popular subjects.

Have you ever visited, or would you like to visit an adventure park in France?

Once you have watched the video, have a discussion and find out which one is likely to be the most popular in your class, and why.

Le savais-tu?

Adventure parks offer an attractive family holiday, as they provide an exciting range of activities. Two of the most popular, Disneyland Paris and Parc Astérix, are approximately 30 km from Paris, but there is a good variety of exciting adventure parks all over France and in other Francophone countries. There are about 200 in France alone, and the average French person visits an adventure park three times a year.

1 Associe les thèmes et les parcs.
Match the subjects with the parks.

1 l'histoire
2 les sciences
3 les volcans
4 la mer
5 les bandes dessinées

a Vulcania
b Marineland
c Le Puy du Fou
d Le Parc Astérix
e La Cité de l'espace

2 Associe les images et les phrases.
Match the pictures with the sentences.

1

Cap Jaseux au Canada

2

Juraparc en Suisse

3

Aqwaland en Martinique

4

Carthage Land en Tunisie

a J'adore les animaux sauvages.
b L'histoire ancienne, c'est ma passion.
c Je voudrais faire du sport en montagne.
d J'aime aller à la piscine.

Module 4: Ta mission...

- Describe what sort of area places are in
- Say where places are
- Ask questions using *quel(le)*, *quand* and *où*
- Use *aller* to talk about the future
- Talk about being hungry, thirsty or scared
- Use intensifiers
- Say what I might do at a *colonie de vacances*
- Understand simple instructions
- Talk about other French-speaking countries
- Describe the weather
- Say more about what I'm going to do and what I'd like to do
- Talk about holidays

Objectifs
- Describe what sort of area places are in
- Say where places are

Langue et grammaire

Using à
In Module 1 you used *à* to mean 'in' with the name of a town. It can also mean 'to':

Je suis à Paris. — I am in Paris.
Je vais à Marseille. — I am going to Marseille.
You can use *à* whether you are staying or going.

Compass directions
To say whether a place is in the north, south, west or east, use:

dans le nord — in the north
dans le sud — in the south
dans l'ouest — in the west
dans l'est — in the east

Using *on*
You have met the word *on* before. In this topic, it is used like a general 'you':

On voit la Seine. — You see the river Seine.
Even when it means 'you' it still takes the same form as with *il* or *elle*.

Je vais en ville. — I'm going into town.
Il/elle va en ville. — He/she's going into town.
On va en ville. — You're going into town.

---

1 Lis le quiz. Pour chaque phrase, choisis *d'accord* ou *pas d'accord*.
Read the quiz. For each sentence, choose d'accord *or* pas d'accord.

Connais-tu la géographie de la France? Fais le quiz.

1 Lille est dans le nord de la France.

2 Nantes est dans l'ouest de la France.

3 Quand on est à Paris, on voit la Loire.

4 Strasbourg est dans l'est de la France.

5 Toulouse est dans le nord-est de la France.

6 Quand on va à Nice, on va au bord de la mer.

7 La Seine, la Loire et le Rhône sont des montagnes.

8 Quand on est dans le Massif Central, on est à la montagne.

2 À deux, trouvez les endroits mentionnés dans le quiz.
In pairs, find all the places mentioned in the quiz.

Exemple

A Où est Lille?   **B** Voilà Lille, dans le nord.

3 Écoute et corrige tes réponses au quiz.
Listen and correct your answers to the quiz.

4 Complète les phrases en français.
Complete the sentences in French.

a 1 Nice est dans le _____ de la France.

2 La Dordogne est dans _____ de la France.

3 Lille est une _____ dans le nord de la France.

4 Toulouse est dans le _____ de la France.

5 Les Pyrénées sont des _____ dans le sud de la France.

b 1 Nantes est _____ de la France.

2 Strasbourg _____ l'est de la France.

3 Quand on est en Bretagne, on est _____ France.

4 Quand on est en Ardèche, _____ à la campagne.

Vocabulaire	
le nord	north
le sud	south
l'est	east
l'ouest	west
le fleuve	river
au bord de la mer	at/to the seaside
à la montagne	in the mountains
en ville	in town/in the city
d'accord	I agree, OK!
pas d'accord	I disagree
quand	when

5 À deux. A choisit une destination. B pose des questions pour deviner où va A.
In pairs. A chooses a destination. B asks questions to guess where A is going.

Exemple
B Tu vas à la montagne?   **A** Non.   **B** Tu vas au bord de la mer?

1 La Seine à Paris   **2** La montagne, dans les Pyrénées   **3** Le bord de la mer, à Nice   **4** La campagne, en Ardèche

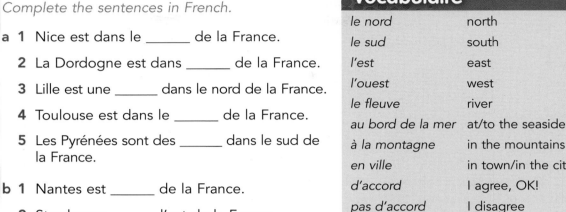

6 Fais des recherches et écris trois ou quatre autres questions pour le quiz.
Do some research and write three or four more questions for the quiz.

7 Fais des recherches et écris un exposé sur une région de France. ⭐
Do some research and write a presentation about a region of France.

Voie express

Make sure you know how to say where places are. You need to make sure you can use *on* and understand different meanings depending on the context because French people use *on* very often. If you find you can do the quiz very easily, you could try writing an article about a region of France. Include interesting information about its geographical features. You might have to do some research first and find some pictures to illustrate your article.

Objectifs
- Ask questions using *quel(le)*, *quand* and *où*
- Use *aller* to talk about the future

Langue et grammaire

Asking questions

One useful word when asking questions in French is *quel(le)*. Use *quel* with a masculine word and *quelle* with a feminine word:

C'est quel genre de parc?	What kind of park is it?
C'est quelle saison?	Which season is it?

Although the masculine and the feminine forms are spelled differently, they are pronounced the same. *Quand?* and *où?* are also very useful words when asking questions in French.

Tu vas où?	Where are you going?
Tu vas quand?	When are you going?

Using *aller* to talk about the future

A simple way of expressing the future in French is to use *aller* in the present tense followed by the infinitive of the verb you want to use:

Je vais aller à Disneyland.	I'm going to go to Disneyland
Ça va être sympa!	It's going to be nice!

Pronunciation

Remember, when a verb ends in *–ent*, the ending is not pronounced. For example, *ils aiment*.

---

1 Lis les SMS et trouve l'équivalent français de:

Read the text messages and find the French for:

1 Where are you going to go?

2 When are you going to go?

3 What type of park is it?

4 What region is it in?

> Tu vas aller où?
>
> Je vais aller à Vulcania…
>
> C'est quel genre de parc?
>
> C'est pour les personnes qui aiment les volcans.
>
> C'est dans quelle région?
>
> C'est dans le Massif Central.
>
> Tu vas y aller quand?
>
> Au printemps… en avril.

Le parc Vulcania

cone © Luc Olivier 2010

---

2 À deux. A regarde la carte et pose des questions. B répond aux questions.

In pairs. A looks at the map and asks questions. B replies to the questions.

Exemple   **A** Marineland, c'est dans quelle région?

   B C'est dans le sud.

1 Vulcania   **2** Marineland   **3** Puy du Fou

4 Cité de l'espace   **5** Disneyland

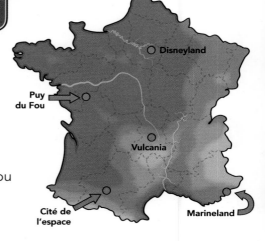

3 Associe les images et les descriptions.

Match the pictures and the descriptions.

1  **2**  **3**  **4**  **5**

a C'est pour les personnes qui aiment la mer.

b C'est pour les personnes qui aiment les montagnes russes.

c C'est pour les personnes qui aiment l'espace.

d C'est pour les personnes qui aiment l'histoire.

e C'est pour les personnes qui aiment les volcans.

4 Écoute. Dans quel ordre est-ce que tu entends les questions?

Listen. In what order do you hear the questions?

a What sort of park is it?		**b** What region is it in?	
c When are you going?		**d** Where are you going?	

5 Écoute, puis lis les phrases. Vrai ou faux?

Listen then read the statements. True or false?

1 Lucas va aller à Marineland.

2 Juillet, c'est en été.

3 Justine va aller à la Cité de l'espace.

4 La Cité de l'espace, c'est à Toulouse.

5 L'anniversaire de Justine, c'est au printemps.

6 Félix va aller au Puy du Fou en automne.

7 Sophie et Abdou vont aller à Disneyland.

6 À deux. B choisit un parc et une saison. A pose les questions de l'exercice 4. Ensuite, changez de rôle.

In pairs. B chooses a park and a season. A asks the questions from exercise 4. Then swap roles.

Exemple

A Tu vas aller où?   **B** Je vais aller au parc Astérix.

7 Écris un résumé du dialogue. ⭐

Write a summary of your dialogue.

Vocabulaire

Tu vas aller…	You are going to go…
Je vais aller…	I am going to go…
Quel genre de parc?	What kind of park?
les montagnes russes	rollercoasters
pour les personnes qui aiment…	for people who like…
quelle région?	which area?
au printemps	in the spring
en été	in the summer
en automne	in the autumn
en hiver	in the winter
Ça va être…	It's going to be…

Voie express

The most important thing in this topic is learning to express things that you are going to do in the future. Pay special attention to the explanation of how to use *aller* to say what you are going to do and how to ask others what they are going to do.

Objectifs
- Talk about being hungry, thirsty or scared
- Use intensifiers

Langue et grammaire

Talking about being hungry, thirsty or scared

To say you are hungry, thirsty or scared, use the verb *avoir*:

J'ai faim.	I'm hungry.
J'ai soif.	I'm thirsty.
J'ai peur.	I'm scared.

To say you are not hungry, thirsty or scared, use the phrase *je n'ai pas*. Remember that *ne* always comes before the verb and *pas* always comes after:

*Je **n'**ai **pas** faim.* I'm not hungry.

To ask friends if they are hungry, thirsty or scared, use *Tu as…?*

Tu as soif?	Are you hungry?

Or you could use *Tu n'as pas…?*:

Tu n'as pas peur?	Aren't you scared?

Remember that when you ask a question in French your voice must go up at the end. Listen carefully to the audio and copy the intonation when you ask questions.

Intensifiers

If you want to provide a more precise answer, you can add phrases such as *pas du tout* (not at all), *un peu* (a little), *très* (very) or *trop* (too or too much):

J'ai très soif.	I am very thirsty.
Je n'ai pas du tout faim.	I am not hungry at all.

1 Trouve une deuxième bulle pour chaque personne.
Find a second bubble for each person.

1 J'ai faim!

2 J'ai soif!

3 J'ai peur!

a Au secours!   b Je voudrais un sandwich.   c H₂O Je voudrais de l'eau.

2 Écoute pour vérifier tes réponses à l'exercice 1 et répète les phrases.
Listen to check your answers to exercise 1 and repeat the sentences.

3 Associe les paires de phrases. Il y a deux phrases a–j pour les phrases 1–5.
Match the pairs of sentences. There are two sentences from the list a–j for each sentence 1–5.

1 Oui, j'ai faim.	**a** Une limonade? Non, merci.	**b** Je voudrais un sandwich.
2 Oui, j'ai peur.	**c** Au secours!	**d** Je voudrais de l'eau.
3 Non, je n'ai pas soif.	**e** Ça va bien.	**f** Je déteste les dinosaures.
4 Non, je n'ai pas peur.	**g** Je voudrais une salade mixte.	**h** Je voudrais un jus d'orange.
5 Oui, j'ai soif.	**i** De l'eau? Non, merci.	**j** Les monstres de la mer, génial!

4 À deux. A pose une question. B répond avec des phrases de l'exercice 3.
In pairs. A asks a question. B responds with sentences from exercise 3.

Exemple
A Tu as peur?   **B** Oui, j'ai peur. Au secours!

Tu as faim?   Tu as soif?   Tu as peur?

5 Écoute et note l'ordre des mots.
Listen and number the words in the order you hear them.

a très   **b** trop   **c** un peu   **d** pas du tout   **e** assez

6 Écoute et choisis la bonne option.
Listen and choose the correct ending.

1 Abdou is…   **a** very hungry.   **b** quite hungry.

2 Sophie is…   **a** not at all thirsty.   **b** very thirsty.

3 Nicolas is…   **a** quite scared.   **b** too scared.

Vocabulaire

J'ai faim.	I am hungry.
J'ai soif.	I am thirsty.
J'ai peur.	I am scared.
Au secours!	Help!
Je voudrais…	I would like…
la salade mixte	mixed salad
le dinosaure	dinosaur
le monstre	monster

7 a Choisis une image, et écris un dialogue. ⭐
Choose a picture and write a dialogue.

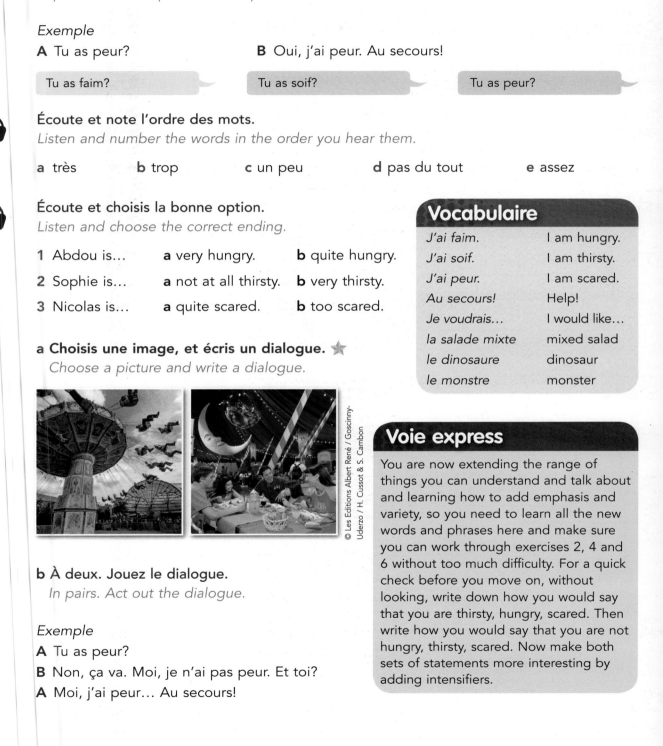

© Les Editions Albert René / Goscinny-Uderzo / H. Cussot & S. Cambon

b À deux. Jouez le dialogue.
In pairs. Act out the dialogue.

Exemple
A Tu as peur?
B Non, ça va. Moi, je n'ai pas peur. Et toi?
A Moi, j'ai peur… Au secours!

Voie express

You are now extending the range of things you can understand and talk about and learning how to add emphasis and variety, so you need to learn all the new words and phrases here and make sure you can work through exercises 2, 4 and 6 without too much difficulty. For a quick check before you move on, without looking, write down how you would say that you are thirsty, hungry, scared. Then write how you would say that you are not hungry, thirsty, scared. Now make both sets of statements more interesting by adding intensifiers.

Objectifs
- Say what I might do at a *colonie de vacances*
- Understand simple instructions

Langue et grammaire

Plural verbs

In formal French, use *nous* to mean 'we'. Verbs that come after *nous* end in *–ons*.

nous proposons	we offer / we are offering

In less formal contexts, use *on* to mean 'we':

on joue	we play / we are playing

Use *ils* (or *elles* for groups which are all female) to mean 'they'. The verb usually ends in *–ent*.

ils/elles jouent	they play / they are playing
ils/elles visitent	they visit / they are visiting

Some irregular verbs end in *–ont*:

ils/elles ont	they have
ils/elles vont	they go / they are going
ils/elles font	they do / they are doing

Using the imperative

To give instructions or advice, you need to use the imperative. Use two different forms:

Informal (people you say *tu* to)

Écoute!	Listen!
Regarde!	Look!
Fais attention!	Be careful!

Formal (people you say *vous* to, or more than one person)

Écoutez!	Listen!
Regardez!	Look!
Faites attention!	Be careful!

À PROJET-COLO, nous proposons:

1 un séjour multi-activités à la campagne

Pour les 12–14 ans

Ils font des balades en forêt, ils jouent au tennis ou au mini-golf. Ils font aussi de l'équitation. Le soir, ils font des jeux, ils jouent aux cartes ou ils chantent. C'est un séjour très sympa.

2 un séjour nautique au bord de la mer

Pour les 12–15 ans

Ils vont à la plage et ils jouent au beach-volley. Ils font aussi de la natation ou de la plongée sous-marine. Ils font de la voile ou de la planche à voile. C'est un séjour très amusant.

3 un séjour linguistique à Londres

Pour les 12–17 ans

Le matin, ils ont des cours d'anglais. L'après-midi, ils visitent les monuments de Londres. Ils vont à Oxford et à Canterbury. C'est un séjour très intéressant.

1

a Les phrases suivantes décrivent quelle colo?
Which *colo* do the following sentences describe?

1 They play tennis.

2 They stay at the seaside.

4 They are in the countryside.

5 They visit the sights of London.

7 They can play cards in the evening.

b Traduis les phrases en français.
Translate the sentences into French.

3 They can go windsurfing.

6 They have English classes.

2 Choisis une bonne colo pour chaque personne.
Choose a suitable summer camp for each person.

Je n'aime pas aller au bord de la mer. Je voudrais apprendre l'anglais.

J'aime les vacances à la campagne. Je voudrais faire de l'équitation.

J'adore la natation et les sports nautiques. Je voudrais faire de la plongée sous-marine.

Voie express

As well as using verbs in the singular form you need to learn how to use them in the plural form and how to understand instructions. This topic is very important and you should work through all of it to make sure you understand and can use these verb forms. It is something that lots of people find difficult, so don't worry if you don't get it straight away.

3 Écoute. Trouve trois différences avec les bulles de l'exercice 2. Écris en français.
Listen. Find three differences with the bubbles in exercise 2. Write them in French.

4 Fais un sondage dans la classe. Quelle colo est la plus populaire?
Do a survey of the class. Which is the most popular holiday camp?

5 **a** Dans quel ordre est-ce que tu entends ces instructions?
Number the bubbles according to the order you hear them in.

a Arrête!

b Fais attention!

c Attrape le ballon!

d Allez dans la forêt!

e Écoute bien la musique!

f Regardez le monument!

b Associe les images et les bulles.
Match the pictures and the bubbles.

1  2

3 4

5 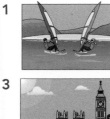 6

Vocabulaire

proposer	to offer
jouer aux cartes	to play cards
faire de l'équitation	to go horse riding
faire des jeux	to play games
faire de la natation	to swim
avoir des cours	to have lessons
un séjour	a stay
ils vont	they go
apprendre	to learn
attraper le ballon	to catch the ball
à la plage	to the beach
la plongée sous-marine	scuba diving
la voile	sailing
la planche à voile	windsurfing

6 Écris un bref exposé sur ta colo idéale, ou fais une liste. ⭐
Write a short presentation about your ideal holiday camp, or make a list of its characteristics.

Objectifs
- Talk about other French-speaking countries
- Describe the weather

Langue et grammaire

Talking about the weather

To ask what the weather is like, use:
Quel temps fait-il?
You rarely need the word *temps* in the answer.
Instead say:

Il fait chaud.	It's hot.
Il fait froid.	It's cold.
Il fait beau.	The weather is nice.
Il fait mauvais.	The weather is bad.
Il y a du soleil.	It's sunny.
Il pleut.	It's raining.
Il neige.	It's snowing.

Talking about countries

To introduce the name of a country or a continent, use:
- *en* with feminine names of countries or continents

Le Sénégal est en Afrique.   Senegal is in Africa.
Ben va aller en France.   Ben is going to go to France.

- *au* with masculine names of countries

Montréal est au Canada.   Montreal is in Canada.
Abdou va aller au Sénégal.   Abdou is going to go to Senegal.
Unlike in English, you use the same preposition to say both where you are and where you are going to.

1 Écoute et mets les phrases dans le bon ordre.
Listen to the audio and put the sentences in the right order.

Exemple

c, …

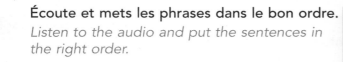

a Bah, oui, il fait froid!

b Il pleut! Et il fait froid?

c Salut, Marie, ça va à Dakar?

d Oh, c'est nul! Viens à Dakar!

e Arrête! Ici, il fait mauvais. Il pleut, comme d'habitude.

f Il fait beau. Il y a du soleil, comme d'habitude.

g J'y pense…

h Pas trop mal. Quel temps fait-il au Sénégal?

i Super! Et toi, Abdou?

2 Relis les bulles de l'exercice 1. Trouve l'équivalent français de:
Reread the speech bubbles from exercise 1. Find the French for:

1 What is the weather like in Senegal?   **2** The weather's nice.   **3** It's sunny.

4 It's raining.   **5** It's cold.   **6** The weather's bad.

3 À deux. Jouez le dialogue de l'exercice 1.
In pairs. Act out the dialogue from exercise 1.

4 Déchiffre les anagrammes et recopie le dialogue correctement.
Solve the anagrams and rewrite the dialogue correctly.

Lucas et son cousin Hugo à Montréal, au Canada:

L Salut, Hugo. Il fait quel **spemt** au Canada?   **H** Il **tiaf** très froid. Il **genie**. Et toi, Lucas?

L Ça va. Il y a du **liosel**.   **H** Et il fait **haduc**?   **L** Non, pas vraiment!

5 À deux, imaginez un dialogue entre Dan, à Manchester, et sa grand-mère en France.
In pairs, prepare and act out a dialogue between Dan in Manchester and his grandmother in France.

6 **a** Lis l'article en français, puis les phrases en anglais. Vrai ou faux? ⭐
Read the article in French, then the statements in English. True or false?

1 Senegal is in North Africa.

2 There are four seasons in Senegal.

3 The rainy season starts in June.

4 December is in the rainy season.

Vocabulaire

J'y pense.	I'm thinking about it.
viens	come
comme d'habitude	as usual
pas trop mal	not too bad
pas vraiment	not really
environ	about
par an	per year
entre	between
exister	to exist
seulement	only
rarement	rarely
la saison des pluies	the rainy season
la saison sèche	the dry season

Le climat du Sénégal

Sénégal
Dakar

Le Sénégal est en Afrique de l'ouest. Il fait beau et chaud: il y a environ 3000 heures de soleil par an! À Dakar, la température varie entre 24° et 30°.

Le printemps, l'été, l'automne, l'hiver, ça n'existe pas au Sénégal. Il y a seulement deux saisons:
- **la saison des pluies**
  (en juin, juillet, août, septembre, octobre, il pleut beaucoup)
- **la saison sèche**
  (en novembre, décembre, janvier, février, mars, avril, mai, il pleut rarement).

Il pleut à Dakar.

b Lis l'article et réponds aux questions en français.
Read the article and answer the questions in French.

1 Où est le Sénégal exactement?

2 Il y a combien de saisons au Sénégal?

3 Il fait quel temps en juillet au Sénégal?

4 La saison sèche commence quand au Sénégal?

Voie express

Do you know anyone who has been to a part of the world where French is spoken other than France? If you do, tell the rest of the class what you know, using some of the vocabulary here to help you. You should start to build up your knowledge of the whole French-speaking world. Exercise 6 will show you techniques for working out the meaning of unfamiliar language, which will help speed up your progress.

Objectifs
- Say more about what I'm going to do and what I'd like to do
- Talk about holidays

Langue et grammaire

Using *aller*

You have already learned to use the present tense of *aller* followed by a verb in the infinitive to say what you are going to do:

Je vais jouer au foot. I'm going to play football.

You can use other forms of the verb *aller* to describe what other people plan to do:

je vais	I'm going
tu vas	you're going
il/elle va	he/she/it is going
on va	we're going (informal)
nous allons	we're going
vous allez	you're going
ils/elles vont	they're going
Qu'est-ce que tu vas faire?	What are you going to do?

Je voudrais

To say what you'd like to do, use *je voudrais* followed by a verb in the infinitive:

Je voudrais aller au Maroc. I'd like to go to Morocco.

Remember that you can also use *je voudrais* followed by a noun:

Je voudrais un sandwich. I'd like a sandwich.

Pronunciation

Remember that 'th' always sounds like the letter 't' in French, so be careful when you say *un thé à la menthe.*

Écoute et lis.
Listen and read.

2 Travaillez à deux. Trouvez l'équivalent français dans l'exercice 1.
Work in pairs. Find the French equivalent in exercise 1.

1 with my parents

2 without my parents

3 It's going to be brilliant.

4 It's going to be rubbish.

5 You're going to eat tagines.

6 I'd like to go to the desert.

7 What are you going to do this summer?

8 I am going to spend two weeks at the seaside.

Vocabulaire

partir	to go away, leave
passer	to spend
nager	to swim
dans la mer	in the sea
sur la plage	on the beach
le thé à la menthe	mint tea
sans	without

3 Trouve une expression du texte de l'exercice 1 pour chaque image.
Find a phrase from the text in exercise 1 for each picture.

a  b  c  d 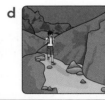 e

4 Écoute les deux conversations. Quelles images de l'exercice 3 illustrent chaque conversation?
Listen to the two conversations. Which pictures from exercise 3 illustrate each conversation?

5 À deux, choisissez deux images de l'exercice 3 et imaginez un dialogue.
In pairs, choose two pictures from exercise 3 and invent a dialogue.

6 Copie la carte du Maroc. Fais un projet pour un voyage en famille. Écris où tu voudrais aller.
Copy out the map of Morocco. Draw a route for a tour that you would like make with your family. Label your planned route with where you would like to go.

Exemple
Je voudrais aller dans le sud.

Voie express

Make sure you know all the different forms of *aller*. You should be confident with the difference between saying you are going to do something and saying you would like to do something. If you are able to complete all the exercises quickly and well, have another look at the story from exercise 1 and write your own conversation in which someone complains about their holiday plans. Try to make it funny!

Langue et grammaire

Places and directions

When used with the name of a city, the word *à* can mean 'in' or 'to':

Je suis à Paris.   I am in Paris.
Je vais à Marseille.   I am going to Marseille.

Use these phrases to describe a location:

dans le nord	in the north
dans le sud	in the south
dans l'ouest	in the west
dans l'est	in the east
au bord de la mer	at the seaside
à la campagne	in the countryside
en ville	in the town/city

Use *en* with feminine countries and continents and *au* with masculine countries and continents:

Le Sénégal est en Afrique.   Senegal is in Africa.
Il va aller au Sénégal.   He is going to go to Senegal.

Using *on* as a general 'you'

The word *on* can be used as a general 'you':
On voit la Seine.   You see the river Seine.

Asking questions

Use *quel* with a masculine word and *quelle* with a feminine word to mean 'which' or 'what':

C'est quel genre de parc?   What kind of park is it?
C'est quelle saison?   Which season is it?

Quand (when) and *où* (where) are also very useful for asking questions.

Tu vas où?   Where are you going?
Tu vas quand?   When are you going?

Using *aller* to talk about the future

For a simple way to express the future, use *aller* in the present tense and a verb in the infinitive:

Je vais aller au Maroc.   I'm going to go to Morocco.
Ça va être bien.   It's going to be good.

Saying what you would like to do

To say what you'd like to do, use *je voudrais* and a verb in the infinitive:

Je voudrais aller à Dakar.   I'd like to go to Dakar.

You can also use *je voudrais* with a noun:
Je voudrais un sandwich.   I'd like a sandwich.

Talking about being hungry, thirsty or scared

To say you are hungry, thirsty or scared, use *avoir*. For a precise answer, add *pas du tout* (not at all), *un peu* (a little), *très* (very) or *trop* (too or too much):

J'ai très soif.   I am very thirsty.
Tu n'as pas peur?   Aren't you scared?
Je n'ai pas du tout faim.   I am not hungry at all.

Ils and *elles*

Remember that after *ils* or *elles*, the verb usually ends in *–ent*:

ils/elles jouent   they play / are playing

However, some irregular verbs end in *–ont*:

ils/elles ont   they have
ils/elles vont   they go / are going
ils/elles font   they do / are doing

Using the imperative

To give instructions or advice, use the imperative:

	Informal (people you say *tu* to)	Formal (people you say *vous* to)
Listen!	*Écoute!*	*Écoutez!*
Be careful!	*Fais attention!*	*Faites attention!*

Talking about the weather

To ask what the weather is like, say:
Quel temps fait-il?

You can answer like this:

Il fait froid.	It's cold.
Il fait beau.	The weather is nice.
Il y a du soleil.	It's sunny.

Vocabulaire

La géographie
quelle région?
le nord
le sud
l'est
l'ouest
à la plage
au bord de la mer
à la montagne
en ville
dans la mer
sur la plage

Les saisons
au printemps
en été
en automne
en hiver

La faim, la soif et la peur
J'ai faim.
J'ai soif.
J'ai peur.

Le temps
Quel temps fait-il?
Il fait froid.
Il fait chaud.
Il fait beau.
Il fait mauvais.
Il y a du soleil.
Il pleut.
Il neige.
la saison des pluies
la saison sèche

Les opinions
J'y pense.
C'est…
nul
génial
super
sympa
comme d'habitude
pas trop mal
pas vraiment
(pas) d'accord

Les mots utiles
une semaine
un an
Connais-tu…?
Au secours!
sans
avec
entre
environ
seulement
rarement
Je voudrais…
boire
passer
partir
apprendre
proposer
exister

En vacances
un séjour
jouer aux cartes
faire des ballades

faire de l'équitation
faire des jeux
faire de la natation
avoir des cours
attraper le ballon
nager
la plongée sous-marine
la planche à voile
les montagnes russes
le parc

Les impressions
on est
on voit
on aime
on déteste

Mission accomplie?

I can…

- [ ] Describe what sort of area places are in
- [ ] Say where places are
- [ ] Ask questions using *quel(le)*, *quand* and *où*
- [ ] Use *aller* to talk about the future
- [ ] Talk about being hungry, thirsty or scared
- [ ] Use intensifiers

- [ ] Say what I might do at a *colonie de vacances*
- [ ] Understand simple instructions
- [ ] Talk about other French-speaking countries
- [ ] Describe the weather
- [ ] Say more about what I'm going to do and what I'd like to do
- [ ] Talk about holidays

Le Futuroscope

A Le Futuroscope est un parc pour les personnes qui aiment le multimédia et les nouvelles technologies.

B Le Futuroscope est à Poitiers, dans l'ouest de la France.

C C'est ouvert tous les jours du 16 février au 15 septembre. Du 15 septembre au 5 janvier, le Futuroscope est ouvert le week-end et pendant les vacances scolaires.

D En hiver, le parc est fermé du 6 janvier au 15 février.

1 **Lis l'article sur le Futuroscope. Trouve la bonne question pour chaque partie du texte.**
Read the article on Futuroscope. Find the right question for each part of the text.

1 C'est où?   **2** C'est ouvert quand?   **3** C'est ouvert en hiver?   **4** C'est quel genre de parc?

2 **Lis l'article encore une fois. Trouve le contraire de:**
Read the article again. Find the opposite of:

1 les personnes qui détestent   **2** dans l'est   **3** c'est fermé   **4** en été

3 **Écoute le dialogue et complète les blancs.**
Listen to the dialogue and fill in the gaps.

A Le Futuroscope, c'est **a** *quel* genre de parc?

B C'est pour les gens qui **b** _____ les nouvelles technologies.

A Et c'est **c** _____?

B C'est à Poitiers, dans l'ouest de la **d** _____.

A C'est ouvert **e** _____?

B C'est ouvert tous les jours du 16 février au 15 **f** _____.

A C'est **g** _____ en hiver?

B C'est fermé du 6 **h** _____ au 15 février.

A OK. Merci.

4 **À deux, jouez le dialogue de l'exercice 3.**
In pairs, act out the dialogue from exercise 3.

Ils parlent du Futuroscope

Les spectacles sont super!
Malik, 12 ans

J'adore le Futuroscope!
Clémentine, 13 ans

Je n'aime pas les nouvelles technologies.
Je ne vais pas retourner au Futuroscope.
Hugo, 14 ans

C'est génial! Je vais y retourner en juillet.
Léa, 14 ans

Je voudrais retourner au Futuroscope.
Pierre, 13 ans

C'est très bien!
Madina, 13 ans

Je recommande ce parc!
Kadija, 13 ans

Je n'aime pas «Les Yeux Grands Fermés»…
J'ai peur dans le noir…
Théo, 11 ans

5 **Lis les commentaires. Qui dit quoi?**
Read the comments. Who says what?

| Malik | Clémentine | Hugo | Léa | Pierre | Madina | Théo | Kadija |

1 It's very good.
2 I'll go back in July.
3 The shows are great.
4 I'm scared in the dark.
5 I recommend this park.
6 I love Futuroscope.
7 I won't go back to Futuroscope.
8 I'd like to go back to Futuroscope.

6 **A va aller au Futuroscope. B pose les questions. A répond. Ensuite changez de rôles.**
A is going to Futuroscope. B asks the questions. A replies. Then swap parts.

1 Le Futuroscope, c'est quel genre de parc?
2 C'est dans quelle région?
3 Tu vas y aller quand?
4 Pourquoi est-ce que tu vas au Futuroscope?

7 **Crée une affiche en français pour un parc que tu connais.**
Create a poster in French for a park that you know.

Do you know what a haiku is or how to create one? A haiku is a Japanese type of poem with just three lines. Each line has a special number of syllables:

• The first line has five syllables.
• The second line has seven syllables.
• The third line has five syllables.

The idea of a haiku is to capture a mood or feeling. Haikus are often to do with nature or seasons.

Il neige toute la nuit
Dans le jardin noir et blanc
Le silence est d'or
Justine, 12 ans

De l'eau et des arbres
Oasis dans le désert
Et le chameau boit
Félix, 11 ans

L'oiseau ne chante pas
Dans la chaleur de l'été
Comme moi il a soif
Sophie, 12 ans

Viens à la maison
Car il fait trop froid dehors
Beau bonhomme de neige
Lucas, 12 ans

Balade de décembre
Le vent d'hiver est très froid
Mais la lune est belle
Maeva, 12 ans

Il pleut au soleil
L'horizon s'habille
D'un bel arc-en-ciel
Thomas, 11 ans

C'est bientôt le printemps?
Demandent les feuilles et
les fleurs
Il fait trop mauvais
Abdou, 12 ans

Le vent du nord chante
Toutes les feuilles dansent
comme des folles
C'est sympa l'automne
Manon, 11 ans

Pas de planche à voile
La plage est triste et
elle pleure
Au revoir l'été
Lucie, 14 ans

Quel haiku mentionne...
Whose haiku mentions...

a a garden in the snow

b the end of summer

c autumn leaves

d a hot summer

e a snowman

f the spring

g a rainbow

h the desert

i the moon

Quels sont les quatre haikus qui vont avec ces images?
Which four haikus go with these pictures?

a   b   c   d

3 Recopie le tableau et ajoute des mots dans les trois colonnes.
Ensuite, traduis-les en anglais.
Copy the grid and add words from the haikus in each column.
Then translate them into English.

Les mois et les saisons		La nature et les animaux		Le temps	
le printemps	*spring*	le jardin	*garden*	froid	*cold*

4 Trouve les équivalents français dans les haikus.
Find the French for these pieces of haiku.

a silence is golden

b handsome snowman

c the weather's too bad

d the camel is drinking

e the wintry wind

f like crazy

g in the summer's heat

h it's raining in the sun

i the beach is sad

5 À deux, relisez les haikus. Quels sont vos préférés? Pourquoi? Comparez vos réponses.
In pairs, read the haikus again. Which are your favourites? Why? Compare your answers.

6 Traduis ces haikus en français.
Translate these haikus into French.

All the birds are singing

Small leaves on the trees

Hello spring

Where is the water?

The camel and the bird are asking

We are very thirsty

7 Choisis deux images et écris des haikus correspondants. Pour t'aider, emploie les mots des exercices 3, 5 et 7.
Choose two images and write some haikus to go with them. Use the words and phrases from exercises 3, 5 and 7 to help you.

Attrapez-les!

Read the latest episode of the bande dessinée. There are four examples of the imperative. Can you spot them?

1. JE PENSE QUE NOUS SOMMES PRÈS...

2. C'EST DANS QUELLE DIRECTION?

C'EST À DROITE. OH NON, IL PLEUT.

JE PENSE QUE C'EST À GAUCHE.

NON, ON PEUT VOIR LA MAISON. C'EST TOUT DROIT.

3. JE VAIS METTRE ÇA DANS LE SAC DE BLONDIE. EN PRISON, ELLE NE PEUT PAS NOUS ARRÊTER.

AHAHA! ET ALORS, JE PEUX AVOIR MON PARKING!

VOTRE PARKING?

EUH ... NOTRE PARKING BIEN SÛR!

4. AÏE!

5. ÉCOUTEZ! IL Y A QUELQU'UN ICI!

Résumé

Les amis vont chez M. Dupont. Lucas veut écouter la conversation entre M. Dupont et M. Vilain.

La maison est à droite ou à gauche? Les amis ne savent pas. Ça va mal. Il pleut. Finalement, Lucas voit la maison.

Quand les amis arrivent, les hommes parlent de Mme Héros. Elle est une activiste écologique et elle va causer des problèmes Alors, ils ont un plan horrible. Ils vont mettre un liquide mystérieux dans son sac. En prison, elle ne peut pas sauver le parc.

Les amis écoutent. Ils sont bien silencieux, mais…

«Aïe!»

Sophie tombe. Les hommes voient les amis et ils veulent les attraper. Les amis ont peur, donc Manon appelle la police. Elle arrive juste à temps…

Activité

In groups, choose one panel each. Translate the dialogue from your panel into English. Combine your translations to create the whole story.

Pronunciation

Now you have been learning French for a while, you are aware that French sounds very different from English. Even words that look the same in both languages are pronounced differently.

You should always try to pronounce French as accurately as you can. Good pronunciation will help you to understand when you hear people speak French, and will also help French people to understand you!

It is always difficult to learn how to pronounce a new language. Think about people learning English. How do you pronounce these words containing 'ough'?

drought	though	through	rough
thought	Loughborough		

No wonder people can get confused! Some languages even use a different alphabet. Look at how these people write 'hello'.

Think about what you know already:

Reminders

1 If a word ends with a 't', 's', 'd' or 'x', you don't pronounce the last letter:
   petit   *anglais*   *bavard*   *paresseux*

2 If you add an 'e' to make –te, –se or –de, you **do** pronounce the consonant:
   petite   *anglaise*   *bavarde*

3 Accents and marks are used to give information on pronunciation and differentiate confusable words. In French, there are three accents (acute, grave and circumflex) and two marks (trema and cedilla):
   étagère   *forêt*   *naïve*   *ça*

4 Some different combinations of letters sound the same. For example *é* and *ez*:
   été   *regardez*

5 The combination *oi* sounds like 'wa':
   moi

Vowel sounds

au   **eau**   In French, when you combine an 'a' (or 'ea') with an 'u', it sounds like an 'o':
                au Canada   *de l'eau*

ou   The letters 'ou' are pronounced like the vowel sound in the English word 'soup':
                nous   *vous*   *beaucoup*

eu   Also listen out for the sound of the letters 'eu':
                il pleut   *deux*

ai   **ei**   The combinations 'ai' and 'ei' are pronounced the same. Practise saying this sentence aloud:
                Il fait du soleil.

1 Écoute. Tu entends quels mots?
Listen. Which words do you hear?

1 fois   fait   2 joie   j'ai   3 moi   mais   4 soif   Seine

5 toi   tes   6 nuage   neige   7 je vois   je vais

8 C'est François.   C'est français.   9 C'est froid.   C'est frais.

2

a À deux, lisez les mots à voix haute.
In pairs, read the words aloud.

b Répétez chaque mot. C'est quoi en anglais?
Repeat each word. What is the English equivalent?

beau   faux   gâteau   chaud

3 Écoute. Copie et complète les phrases. Cherche les mots inconnus dans un dictionnaire.
Listen. Copy and complete the sentences. Look up any words you don't know in a dictionary or in the glossary.

Bonj_ _r, mon am_ _r!

Je v_ _drais j_ _er p_ _r T_ _l_ _se.

L_ _l_ _ est f_ _? Pas du t_ _t!

D_ _ze b_ _les rouges! P_ _rquoi?

4 À deux, répétez les phrases de l'exercice 3. De plus en plus vite!
In pairs, repeat the sentences in exercise 3. Faster and faster!

5 **a** Trouve l'intrus.
Find the odd one out in each line.

b Écoute pour vérifier tes réponses.
Listen to check your answers.

1   bleu   il pleut   beau

2   deux   douze   un jeu

3   Matthieu   les yeux   gâteaux

6 **a** Cherche dans le dictionnaire l'équivalent français de:
Find in the dictionary the French for:

1 nephew   2 bird   3 boat   4 cabbage   5 castle

6 to find   7 game   8 hat   9 high   10 animals

b Devine la prononciation de chaque mot.
Guess the pronunciation of each word.

c Écoute pour vérifier.
Listen to check.

La pyramide du Louvre à Paris

La Joconde, par Léonard de Vinci

La tour Eiffel à Paris

Le musée d'Orsay à Paris

La Seine à Paris

Découverte du monde:

Paris is the capital city of France and it is a very popular destination for tourists. Have you ever been there, or would you like to go? Do you know what you would like to see and do in Paris?

Once you have watched the video and seen the places mentioned, have a class discussion. Which ideas are the most appealing to your class and why?

Le savais-tu?

Le musée d'Orsay, one of the most popular museums in Paris, is on the left (south) bank of the Seine. It was originally built as a railway station at the end of the nineteenth century, and reopened as a museum in 1986. It houses an impressive collection of sculptures, photographs and paintings, including works by impressionist and post-impressionist artists such as Claude Monet, Alfred Sisley, Vincent Van Gogh and Paul Cézanne.

1 À deux, regardez les images de Paris.

In pairs, look at the images of Paris. Have you been to any of the places? Which ones would you like to go to?

2 On parle de quoi? Trouve la bonne image pour chaque phrase.

What are they talking about? Find the right picture for each sentence. One doesn't have an image to match. Which one?

a J'ai vu des tableaux impressionnistes.

b J'ai admiré un tableau de Léonard de Vinci.

c Je suis allé au musée du Louvre avec mes parents.

d Je suis monté à la tour Eiffel et j'ai admiré la vue sur Paris.

e J'ai préféré le musée d'art moderne. J'ai trouvé ça très sympa.

Module 5: Ta mission...

- Talk about playing musical instruments
- Give and justify opinions about music
- Describe clothes using a range of adjectives and colours
- Use the verbs *mettre* and *pouvoir*
- Describe objects and positions
- Describe a general impression

- Use familiar words and structures in new contexts
- Use possessive adjectives accurately
- Talk about things I have done using the perfect tense
- Describe a visit to somewhere I have been
- Talk about events in the past using *être* and *avoir* to form the perfect tense
- Accept and turn down invitations

Objectifs
- Talk about playing musical instruments
- Give and justify opinions about music

Langue et grammaire

Jouer

Remember that *jouer* is the French verb 'to play' and that *jouer à* is used to talk about playing a sport or game. To talk about playing a musical instrument, use *jouer de*. Remember to change the *de* depending on whether the musical instrument is masculine or feminine, singular or plural:

- *de + le* changes to *du*
- *de + les* changes to *des*
- *de + la* and *de + l'* do not change.

Je joue du piano.	I play / am playing the piano.
Elle joue des percussions.	She plays / is playing percussion.
Il joue de la guitare.	He plays / is playing the guitar.

To ask a friend what instrument they play, say:

Tu joues de quel instrument? — What instrument do you play / are you playing?

Or if it's clear you are talking about music, just say:

Tu joues de quoi? — What do you play / are you playing?

Pronunciation

Many of the words for musical instruments are the same or similar to the English words, but be careful! They are often pronounced differently. Listen carefully to the pronunciation in the listening exercises.

1 **Regarde les mimes et choisis la bonne lettre (a–h) pour compléter chaque phrase.**
Look at the mimes and choose from phrases a–h to complete each sentence.

1 Sophie...

2 Félix...

3 Justine...

4 Abdou...

a joue du violon.

d joue du saxophone.

b joue de la flûte.

e joue de la trompette.

c joue de la guitare.

f joue des percussions.

2 **a** Écoute pour vérifier tes réponses à l'exercice 1.
Listen to check your answers to exercise 1.

b Écoute encore une fois. Tu entends les noms de ces instruments dans quel ordre?
Listen again, and number the instruments in the order you hear them mentioned.

 la flûte

 la guitare

 le piano

 la trompette

 la harpe

 le saxophone

 le violon

 les percussions

a Écoute. Qui dit quoi?

Listen. Who says what?

1 My favourite style of music is reggae.

2 I only listen to classical music.

3 My favourite music is metal.

4 I don't like rap at all.

b Écoute encore. Trouve et écris en français:

Listen again. Find and write in French:

1 one positive comment

2 one negative comment

3 one comment from somebody who listens to just one kind of music

4 one comment from someone interested in all kinds of music

Lis le blog de Sophie. Vrai ou faux?

Read Sophie's blog. True or false?

1 Les amis sont dans un groupe.

2 Maeva ne joue pas de violon.

3 Tous les amis aiment la musique rock.

4 Sophie écoute un peu de tout.

5 Abdou n'aime pas le reggae.

Vocabulaire

le piano	piano
le violon	violin
la flûte	flute
la harpe	harp
le saxophone	saxophone
la trompette	trumpet
le clavier	keyboard
les percussions (f)	percussion
le blues	blues
le R&B	R&B
le rock	rock
le reggae	reggae
le métal	metal
le hip hop	hip-hop
un instrument de musique	musical instrument
un genre	style, type
un peu de tout	a bit of everything
surtout	especially
classique	classical
par contre	on the other hand
en fait	in fact

Voie express

Make sure you know the difference between jouer *au/à la/à l'/aux* for sports and games and jouer *du/de la/de l'/des* for talking about musical instruments. Practise by using a dictionary to find the names of other games and instruments and make a list beginning each one with *jouer à* or *jouer de* in the correct form.

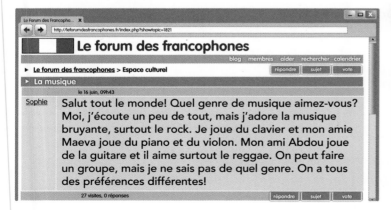

Le forum des francophones

blog   membres   aider   rechercher   calendrier

▶ **Le forum des francophones** > **Espace culturel**   répondre   sujet   vote

▶ **La musique**

le 16 juin, 09h43

Sophie — **Salut tout le monde! Quel genre de musique aimez-vous? Moi, j'écoute un peu de tout, mais j'adore la musique bruyante, surtout le rock. Je joue du clavier et mon amie Maeva joue du piano et du violon. Mon ami Abdou joue de la guitare et il aime surtout le reggae. On peut faire un groupe, mais je ne sais pas de quel genre. On a tous des préférences différentes!**

27 visites, 0 réponses   répondre   sujet   vote

Fais un sondage. Pose des questions sur la musique.

Do a survey. Ask people about their tastes in music.

Écris un résumé du sondage.

Write a report of your survey.

Objectifs
- Describe clothes using a range of adjectives and colours
- Use the verbs *mettre* and *pouvoir*

Langue et grammaire

Adjectives

Remember that French adjectives change depending on the noun they describe. Usually, you add an 'e' for feminine nouns and an 's' for plural nouns:

*un tee-shirt **bleu***	a blue tee-shirt
*des tee-shirts **bleus***	blue tee-shirts
*une chaussure **bleue***	a blue shoe
*des chaussures **bleues***	blue shoes

When the adjective already ends in 'e', there is no need to add a second:

*une jupe **jaune***	a yellow skirt

Some adjectives are irregular:

	ms	mpl	fs	fpl
beautiful	*beau*	*beaux*	*belle*	*belles*
white	*blanc*	*blancs*	*blanche*	*blanches*

Pouvoir + infinitive

Pouvoir means 'to be able to'. You met the phrase *on peut* (we can) in Module 3. Here are some more forms of this verb:

je peux	I can	*il/elle peut*	he/she can
tu peux	you can	*on peut*	we can

You can follow any of these phrases with a verb in its infinitive form (how it's written in the dictionary):

Je peux aller au parc.   I can go to the park.

Mettre

Mettre means 'to put on' or 'to wear':

je mets	I put on / wear
tu mets	you put on / wear
il/elle met	he/she puts on / wears
on met	we put on / wear

---

 1 Trouve la bonne légende pour chaque image.
Find the correct caption for each image.

2 Regarde l'image et trouve un vêtement pour chaque couleur.
Look at the image and find an item of clothing for each of these colours.

> rouge   gris   jaune
> orange
>   vert   noir   marron
>   violet
> blanc   bleu   rose

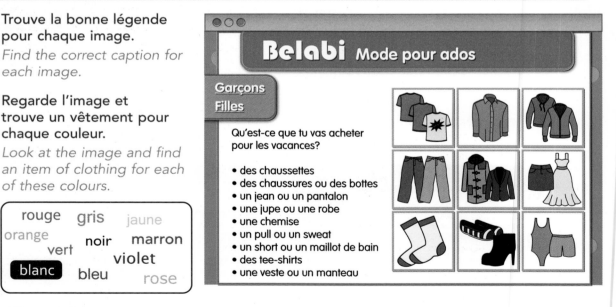

Belabi Mode pour ados

Garçons
Filles

Qu'est-ce que tu vas acheter pour les vacances?

- des chaussettes
- des chaussures ou des bottes
- un jean ou un pantalon
- une jupe ou une robe
- une chemise
- un pull ou un sweat
- un short ou un maillot de bain
- des tee-shirts
- une veste ou un manteau

3 a Écoute. Tu entends ces phrases dans quel ordre?
Listen. Number the sentences in the order you hear them.

a Je regarde des chemises sur Internet.

b Tu préfères le rouge ou le vert?

c Les tee-shirts aussi sont beaux!

d La chemise bleue est très belle.

e Tu ne peux pas mettre ça!

f Qu'est-ce que tu fais?

g Il est trop moche!

h J'adore le jaune!

i Il est très beau!

j Il est moche!

b Écoute encore une fois. Trouve et écris en français:
Listen again. Find and write in French:

1 one sentence to discourage someone from wearing something

2 four sentences to express a positive opinion

3 two sentences to express a negative opinion

4 **Regarde les images, puis complète le dialogue.**
Look at the pictures, and complete the conversation.

Lucas Je ___ un pull ___.

Sa mère Non, tu ne ___ pas ça! C'est ___.

Lucas Alors je ___ un tee-shirt ___.

Sa mère Non, tu peux ___ le sweat ___.

Lucas D'accord je ___ le sweat. J'aime le style skateur.

5 **Le style de Sophie. Lis et réponds aux questions en anglais.**
Sophie's style. Read and answer the questions in English.

Vocabulaire	
la mode	fashion
les ado(lescent)s	teenagers
la chaussette	sock
la chaussure	shoe
les vêtements (m)	clothes
le sweat(-shirt)	sweatshirt
la botte	boot
le jean	jeans
le pantalon	trousers
la jupe	skirt
la robe	dress
la chemise	shirt
le pull	jumper
le short	shorts
le maillot de bain	swimsuit
la veste	jacket
le manteau	winter coat
une tenue	an outfit
beau(x)/belle(s)	beautiful
moche	ugly
mettre	to put on, wear
pouvoir	to be able to

La mode est très importante en France, surtout pour les ados. Les vêtements de sport sont très populaires. Les ados comme moi aiment surtout les vêtements très larges et très longs en style de skateur, parce que c'est cool. Mes parents n'aiment pas cette mode parce qu'ils trouvent ça moche.

a What does Sophie say about fashion in France?

b What do Sophie's parents think about skater fashion?

c How does Sophie describe skater fashion?

d What does Sophie say about sportswear?

e Translate the text.

6 **À trois ou quatre, discutez de vos préférences.**
In threes or fours, talk about what you like to wear and why. Use the dialogue and text in exercises 4 and 5 to help you.

7 **Tu vas à une fête. Décris ta tenue idéale.**
You are going to a party. Describe an ideal outfit.

Voie express

There are a lot of new nouns and adjectives here. Make sure you know the gender of nouns and how to make adjectives agree with them. Both *mettre* and *pouvoir* are important irregular verbs so you need to learn how they behave.

Objectifs
- Describe objects and positions
- Describe a general impression

Langue et grammaire

To describe a scene or a situation, use the phrase *il y a*, meaning 'there is' or 'there are'.

Il y a stays the same whether you are describing one thing or several things.

Il y a un pont.	There is a bridge.
Il y a deux filles.	There are two girls.

You can vary your descriptions by using *on voit* from the verb *voir*, which means 'to see'.

On voit un pont. — We can see a bridge.

To say where something is, use phrases such as:

à gauche — on the left

à droite	on the right
au milieu	in the middle
devant	in front
derrière	behind

Remember to use *je pense que* or *à mon avis* to express your opinion.

Je pense que c'est un beau tableau. — I think it's a beautiful painting.

À mon avis c'est un beau tableau. — In my opinion it's a beautiful painting.

1 **Lis les descriptions. Sophie décrit l'image 1, l'image 2 ou les deux images?**
Read the descriptions. Is Sophie describing picture 1, picture 2 or both?

Petite danseuse de quatorze ans par Edgar Degas

a On voit la tête.

b On voit la main gauche.

c On voit l'oreille gauche.

d On voit le bras gauche.

e On voit le nez et la bouche.

f On voit les pieds et les jambes.

g On voit qu'elle a les cheveux longs.

h On ne voit pas les yeux.

2 **À deux. A décrit une image. B dit si c'est l'image 1, l'image 2 ou les deux images.**
In pairs. A describes one picture. B says whether it's picture 1, picture 2 or both.

Exemple **A** On voit le nez. **B** C'est l'image 1.

Vocabulaire

la tête	head
la main	hand
l'oreille (f)	ear
le bras	arm
le nez	nose
la bouche	mouth
le pied	foot
la jambe	leg
le tableau	painting
à motifs	patterned
le chapeau	hat
le sol	floor
l'herbe	grass
le pont	bridge
la rue	street
le ciel	sky
à gauche	on the left
à droite	on the right
au milieu	in the middle
devant	in front
porter	to wear

3

a Abdou décrit le tableau. Devine quels mots tu vas entendre.
Abdou is describing the painting. Work out which words you'll hear.

> fille   garçon   gris   vert   violet   froid   chaud

b Écoute pour vérifier tes réponses.
Listen to check your answers.

c Réponds aux questions en anglais.
Answer the questions in English.

1 What time of day does Abdou think it is in the painting?

2 What does Abdou think about the painting? Does he seem to like it?

La sieste par Paul Gauguin

4

Complète le texte.
Complete the text.

Au **1** _____, il y a une fille. Elle porte une chemise **2** _____ et une jupe à motifs. Elle a les cheveux longs et **3** _____, et elle porte un chapeau. **4** _____, il y a d'autres filles. Le sol est violet et on peut voir l'herbe verte. On a l'impression qu'il fait **5** _____. Je pense que c'est **6** _____. À mon avis c'est un tableau très **7** _____.

5

Lis le devoir de Lucas. Écris 'vrai' ou 'faux' pour chaque phrase, puis corrige son devoir.
Read Lucas's homework. Write true or false for each sentence, then correct his homework.

> *Le quai Saint-Michel et Notre-Dame* par Maximillien Luce
> 1 À droite, on voit la Seine.
> 2 Au milieu, il y a un pont et à droite il y a une rue.
> 3 Devant le pont, on voit la cathédrale Notre-Dame.
> 4 Le ciel est jaune et il fait beau.
> 5 C'est une scène très colorée.
> 6 Je pense qu'il y a beaucoup de mouvement et d'énergie dans cette photo.

6

À deux. A propose une phrase pour décrire un des tableaux. B dit 'vrai' ou 'faux'.
In pairs. A says one sentence to describe one of the paintings. B says whether it's true or false.

7

Écris une description d'une image de ton choix. ⭐
Write a description of a picture of your choice.

Voie express

In this module, you are extending your range of descriptive language and building your vocabulary. Choose a painting, photograph or other work of art that you like, and prepare a presentation to share with the rest of the class. Try to use a variety of descriptive words to talk about the colours, the shapes, the objects and their positions. Explain in simple words why you like that particular work.

Objectifs
- Use familiar words and structures in new contexts
- Use possessive adjectives accurately

Langue et grammaire

Possessives

You already know how to say 'my' in French: *mon*, *ma* or *mes*. Similarly, the French for 'your' can be either *ton*, *ta* or *tes*.

There is no difference in French between 'his' and 'her'. What is important is the word being described. Study the pattern in the table below.

my	your	his/her
mon frère	*ton frère*	*son frère*
my brother	your brother	his/her brother
ma sœur	*ta sœur*	*sa sœur*
my sister	your sister	his/her sister
mes parents	*tes parents*	*ses parents*
my parents	your parents	his/her parents

Pouvoir and vouloir

You already know that the French for 'I can' is *je peux* from the verb *pouvoir*. You can use it to ask for permission:

Je peux regarder un film?   Can I watch a film?

The French for 'I want' is *je veux* from the verb *vouloir*. It follows a similar pattern:

Si tu veux.   If you like.
Qu'est-ce qu'il veut faire?   What does he want to do?

Pronunciation

Notice, also, the way these verbs are pronounced. The letters *eu* are used a lot in French, so be sure to say them correctly.

Boule et Bill
C'est l'histoire de Boule et de son chien Bill. Son père s'appelle Pierre et sa mère s'appelle Carine.

www.asterix.com © 2013 LES EDITIONS ALBERT RENÉ / GOSCINNY - UDERZO

Astérix et Obélix
Dans le village d'Astérix et d'Obélix, le chef s'appelle Abraracourcix et sa femme s'appelle Bonemine.

© Hergé / Moulinsart 2013

Les aventures de Tintin
Tintin est un jeune journaliste belge. Son chien s'appelle Milou. Ses amis sont le capitaine Haddock et Dupond et Dupont.

1 Lis les descriptions des personnages et trouve l'équivalent français de:
Read through the character descriptions and find the French for:

1 his dog   **2** his father   **3** his mother   **4** his wife   **5** his friends

2 Réponds aux questions en français. Commence chaque phrase par *son, sa* ou *ses*.
Answer the questions in French. Begin each sentence with son, sa or ses.

1 Comment s'appelle le chien de Tintin?   **2** Comment s'appellent les amis de Tintin?

3 Comment s'appellent les parents de Boule?   **4** Comment s'appelle la femme de Abraracourcix?

3 Écoute, puis associe les deux parties des phrases.
Listen then match the beginnings and endings of the sentences.

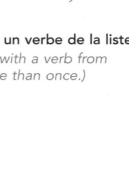

1 Titeuf est   a s'appellent Marie-Rose et Roger.

2 Son meilleur copain s'appelle   b s'appellent Hugo et François.

3 Ses autres copains   c le personnage principal.

4 Sa petite sœur s'appelle   d Manu.

5 Ses parents   e Zizie.

4 À deux. A fait une phrase à propos de Titeuf. B dit si c'est vrai ou faux.
In pairs. A says something about Titeuf. B says whether it is true or false.

5 **a** Écoute. Remplis les blancs avec un verbe de la liste.
Listen to the story. Fill the gaps with a verb from the list. (You will need most more than once.)

veux	peux	peut

1 Je _____ rester ici avec toi?

2 Qu'est-ce que tu _____ faire?

3 Si tu _____.

4 Tu _____ regarder un film avec moi?

5 Je _____ choisir le film?

6 On _____ regarder *Astérix*?

7 Tu _____ aller au lit, s'il te plaît?

b Qui dit chaque phrase 1–7? Abdou (A), son frère (F) ou sa mère (M)?
Who says each line 1–7? Adbou, his brother or his mother?

c Trouve la bonne traduction pour les phrases.
Find the correct translations for the sentences.

   a If you want.

   b Can I choose the film?

   c What do you want to do?

   d Do you want to watch a film with me?

6 Prépare une petite histoire en bande dessinée. Décris les personnages.
Make a cartoon or short comic-strip story. Describe the characters.

Vocabulaire

l'histoire (f)	story
le chien	dog
la femme	wife
le chef	chief
le journaliste	journalist
le meilleur copain	best friend
principal(e)	main
autre	other
jeune	young
belge	Belgian
bien sûr	of course
avec toi	with you
avec moi	with me
aller au lit	to go to bed
vouloir	to want
rester	to stay

Voie express

It is important that you re-use language from earlier in the course as often as possible. Most items of vocabulary and structures can be used in lots of different situations and repetition will help you to remember them. When you are sure you know the difference between *son*, *sa* and *ses*, have a go at a dialogue using the verbs *pouvoir* and *vouloir*.

Objectifs
- Talk about things I have done using the perfect tense
- Describe a visit to somewhere I have been

Langue et grammaire

The perfect tense

To talk about something you saw or did in the past, you use a past tense. One of the most commonly used in French is called the perfect tense. To make the perfect tense, you use the present tense of *avoir* followed by a form of the verb you need to use called the past participle.

To make the past participle of –*er* verbs, remove the –*er* ending and replace it with é.

infinitive	past participle	past perfect tense
regarder	*regardé*	*j'ai regardé*
aimer	*aimé*	*j'ai aimé*

If you want to use the negative form, place *ne … pas* around the part of the verb *avoir*.

je n'ai pas aimé   I didn't like   *je n'ai pas regardé*   I didn't watch

Some irregular verbs have different forms of past participles.

infinitive	past participle	past perfect tense
faire	*fait*	*j'ai fait*
voir	*vu*	*j'ai vu*

Once you know the past participle, you can follow the same rule with *tu, il, elle* and *on*.

tu as aimé   you liked   *il/elle/on a aimé*   he/she/we liked

a Lis le texte sur le Centre Pompidou. Vrai ou faux?
Read the text about the Pompidou Centre. True or false?

b Corrige les phrases fausses.
Correct the statements that are wrong.

Le Centre Pompidou est un musée d'art moderne à Paris.
Les architectes responsables du Centre Pompidou s'appellent Richard Rogers et Renzo Piano.
Richard Rogers est britannique et Renzo Piano est italien.

Bleu, jaune, vert, rouge
Le Centre Pompidou est un bâtiment moderne et très coloré.
Les architectes ont choisi un code couleur simple:
- bleu pour la circulation de l'air (la climatisation)
- jaune pour la circulation électrique
- vert pour la circulation de l'eau
- rouge pour la circulation des personnes (ascenseurs, escalators).

1 The Pompidou Centre is a museum of modern art in Paris.

2 Renzo Piano is a French architect.

3 The other architect is British.

4 The main colours used for the building are blue, yellow, green and red.

5 The architects have used a simple colour code.

6 Blue is for the circulation of water.

7 Yellow is for the circulation of electricity.

8 All lifts and escalators are green.

2 a Écoute les quatre conversations. Qui a fait quoi? Quelle image correspond à quel ami?

Listen to the four conversations. Who did what? Match the picture to the right person.

A  B  C  D

b Écoute encore une fois. Qui a aimé et qui n'a pas aimé le Centre Pompidou? Mets ☺ ou ☹.

Listen again. Who liked the Centre Pompidou and who didn't? Write ☺ or ☹.

3 Remplis les blancs dans le blog de Justine.

Fill the gaps in Justine's blog with words from the list.

écouté	a	aimé	choisi	ai
mangé	trouvé	vu	visité	mangé

Le Forum des Francopho... ✕

http://leforumdesfrancophones.fr/index.php?showtopic=1749

Le forum des francophones

blog membres aider rechercher calendrier

▶ **Le forum des francophones** > **Espace culturel**   répondre sujet vote

▶ Le Centre Pompidou

le 23 juin, 11h27

<u>Justine</u> Ce week-end j'ai _____ Paris. J'_____ adoré le Centre Pompidou. J'ai _____ ça super. J'ai _____ les tableaux de Picasso. On a _____ des musiciens et on _____ regardé des artistes. Après on a _____ dans un restaurant.

---

4 Écris un exposé sur la visite d'un musée ou d'une ville. Utilise les mots ci-dessous pour t'aider.

Write a presentation about a visit to a museum or a town. Use the words below to help you.

J'ai	visité	le musée
On a	vu	des artistes/musiciens
Je n'ai pas	regardé	les tableaux de…
	écouté	dans un restaurant/café
	aimé	des statues
	adoré	la vue sur Paris/Londres/la ville/une fontaine

5 Avec un groupe, présente ton exposé à tes camarades de classe. ⭐

With a group, give your presentation to your classmates. Listen and reward your classmates using the scoring grid.

☺ = bien	☺☺ = très bien	☺☺☺ = excellent	
Name	Pronunciation	Accuracy & fluency	Content & difficulty
LUCAS	☺	☺☺	☺☺

Vocabulaire

britannique	British
italien(ne)	Italian
coloré(e)	colourful
impressionnant(e)	impressive
électrique	electric
le bâtiment	building
la climatisation	air conditioning
l'ascenseur	lift, elevator
le parvis	square, plaza
la fontaine	fountain
la vue	view
la circulation	circulation
la visite	visit
admirer	to admire
choisir	to choose
de toutes les couleurs	in all colours
au dernier étage	on the top floor
vraiment	really

Voie express

Make sure you know what all of the following mean and how to identify them: a verb, the infinitive, the present tense, a past participle. You need to know how to form the past participle of regular verbs ending in *–er* and the past participle of *faire* and *voir*. When you think you can do this, test yourself by writing out ten different things that you did last week.

Objectifs
- Talk about events in the past using *être* and *avoir* to form the perfect tense
- Accept and turn down invitations

Langue et grammaire

The perfect tense with *être*

In the previous topic, you learned how to use the present tense of *avoir* followed by a past participle to say what you did in the past using the perfect tense.

Some common verbs, such as *aller* and *rester*, use the present tense of *être* instead of *avoir* to make the perfect tense. The past participle is formed in the same way.

je suis allé(e)	I went
tu es allé(e)	you went
il est allé	he went
elle est allée	she went
on est allé(e)(s)	we went

Note that you need to add an extra e at the end of the past participle if the action is performed by a girl or a woman.

Ma sœur est allée au concert; mon frère est resté à la maison.
My sister went to the concert; my brother stayed at home.

Making suggestions

When discussing what to do with friends, use *je voudrais* plus an infinitive to introduce what you would like to do, or *on pourrait* to make a suggestion of what you could do.

Je voudrais aller...	I would like to go...
On pourrait regarder...	We could watch...

Le 21 juin, c'est l'été et c'est la fête de la musique! Tous les concerts sont gratuits. Les gens peuvent jouer et écouter tous les styles de musique. Ils peuvent aussi danser et chanter. C'est génial!

Vocabulaire

les gens (m)	people
la chorale	choir
l'année dernière	last year
cette année	this year
un concert	a concert
une compétition	a competition
une soirée	evening
tous/toutes	all
tous les styles	all styles
sortir	to go out
ça commence	it starts
ils peuvent	they can
on pourrait	we could

1 **Lis le texte, puis réponds en anglais.**
Read the text then answer in English.

1 What happens on 21 June?

2 How much does it cost?

3 What can people do? Name four things.

2 **Écoute les interviews, puis écris l'ordre des bulles.**
Listen to the interviews and list the order that you hear the speech bubbles.

a Je suis allée à un concert de musique classique avec mes parents. On a passé une bonne soirée.

b Moi, je suis allé au concert de mon collège et j'ai joué de la guitare. Après on a dansé et on a chanté.

c Je suis restée à la masion avec ma sœur. On a regardé des concerts à la télé.

d Ma sœur est allée à un concert avec ses copains, mais moi, je suis resté à la maison... Cette année, je voudrais sortir.

3 Trouve dans l'exercice 2 l'équivalent français des expressions. Recopie-les.
Find the French for the following phrases in the bubbles. Write down the French phrases.

1 last year   **2** I went   **3** I stayed at home.

4 My sister went to a concert.   **5** I played the guitar.

4 À deux. A demande *Qu'est-ce que tu as fait pour la fête de la musique?* B lit une des bulles de l'exercice 2. A donne le nom de B.
In pairs. A asks what B did for the music festival. B reads one of the bubbles from exercise 2. A says who B is.

Voie express

It is important for now that you know the difference between how to say what you did in the past, using *avoir* with the past participle, and where you went in the past, using *être* with the past participle. Have fun composing a sketch to act out a similar discussion to the one in exercise 6. Try to make it as lively as possible!

5 Choisis la bonne légende pour chaque image.
Choose the right caption for each picture.

a Je voudrais aller au concert de musique classique du collège.

b On pourrait aller à la compétition de street dance près de la tour Eiffel.

c On pourrait aller au concert, place Gambetta.

d On pourrait écouter la chorale de gospel à l'église.

6 **a** Écoute la conversation. Écris a, b, c et d dans le bon ordre quand tu entends les quatre phrases de l'exercice 5.
Listen to the conversation. Write a, b, c and d in the correct order as you hear the four sentences from exercise 5.

b Écoute encore. Qu'est-ce qu'ils ont décidé de faire? Ça commence à quelle heure?
Listen again. What did they decide to do? What time does it start?

7 Prépare un programme pour la fête de la musique. Qu'est-ce que tu voudrais faire? ⭐
Create an imaginary schedule for the music festival. Say what you would like to go to.

Langue et grammaire

Jouer de

To talk about playing a musical instrument, use *jouer de*. Change the *de* depending on the noun:
de + le changes to *du*
de + les changes to *des*
de + la and *de + l'* do not change.

Adjectives

French adjectives change depending on the noun they describe. Usually, you add an 'e' for feminine nouns and an 's' for plural nouns:

un tee-shirt **bleu**	a blue tee-shirt
des tee-shirts **bleus**	blue tee-shirts
une chaussure **bleue**	a blue shoe
des chaussures **bleues**	blue shoes

When the adjective already ends in 'e', there is no need to add a second.

Some adjectives are irregular.

	ms	mpl	fs	fpl
beautiful	*beau*	*beaux*	*belle*	*belles*
white	*blanc*	*blancs*	*blanche*	*blanches*

Pouvoir and *vouloir*

Pouvoir means 'to be able to':

je peux	I can	*tu peux*	you can
il/elle/on peut	he/she/we can		

Vouloir means 'to want':

je veux	I want	*tu veux*	you want
il/elle/on veut	he/she/we want(s)		

You can follow either of these verbs with a verb in its infinitive form:
Je peux regarder un film?

Making suggestions

Use *je voudrais* to say what you would like to do.
Use *on pourrait* to suggest what you could do.
Je voudrais aller au concert.
On pourrait regarder la compétition.

Possessives

Note that there is no difference in French between 'his' and 'her'. The words for 'my', 'your' and 'his/her' all follow the same pattern:

my	your	his/her
mon frère	*ton frère*	*son frère*
ma sœur	*ta sœur*	*sa sœur*
mes parents	*tes parents*	*ses parents*

The perfect tense with *avoir*

To make the perfect tense, you use the present tense of *avoir* followed by a form of the verb you need to use called the past participle. To make the past participle of –er verbs, remove the –er ending and replace it with 'é'. Once you know the past participle, you can follow the same rule with *tu, il, elle* and *on*:

j'ai aimé	I liked
tu as aimé	you liked
il/elle/on a aimé	he/she/we liked

Place *ne … pas* around the *avoir* part to make a negative:

je n'ai pas aimé	I didn't like

Some past participles are irregular:

j'ai fait	I did	*j'ai vu*	I saw

The perfect tense with *être*

Some common verbs use the present tense of *être* instead of *avoir* to make the perfect tense. The past participle is formed in the same way but you need to add an extra 'e' at the end of the past participle if the action is performed by a girl or woman:

aller	rester
je suis allé(e)	*je suis resté(e)*
tu es allé(e)	*tu es resté(e)*
il est resté	*il est allé*
elle est allée	*elle est restée*
on est allé(e)(s)	*on est resté(e)(s)*

Mettre

Mettre means 'to put on' or 'to wear':

je mets	*tu mets*	*il/elle/on met*

Vocabulaire

Les verbes
mettre
porter
pouvoir
vouloir
rester
admirer
choisir
sortir
aller au lit

Les mots utiles
autre
bien sûr
un peu de tout
surtout
par contre
en fait
vraiment
avec toi
avec moi
ça commence
ils peuvent
on pourrait
tous
l'année dernière
cette année
l'histoire

Les couleurs
rouge
bleu(e)
jaune
vert(e)
violet(e)
orange
noir(e)
gris(e)
marron
blanc/blanche
rose

Les descriptions
beau(x)/belle(s)
moche
jeune
belge
britannique
italien(ne)
coloré(e)
de toutes les
couleurs
préféré(e)
impressionnant(e)
électrique
classique
principal
à motifs

La mode
les vêtements (m)
la tenue
la chaussette
la chaussure
le sweat
la botte
le jean
le pantalon
la jupe
la robe
la chemise
le pull
le short
le maillot de bain
la veste
le manteau
le chapeau

Le corps
la tête
la main
l'oreille (f)
le bras
le nez
la bouche
le pied
la jambe

Les positions
à gauche
à droite
au milieu
devant

Les événements
la fête
le concert
la compétition
la soirée
la visite

Au musée
le bâtiment
la climatisation
l'ascenseur
la piazza
le tableau
la fontaine
la vue
la circulation
le sol
au dernier étage
l'herbe
le pont
la rue
le ciel

La musique
le piano
le violon
la flûte
la harpe
la guitare
le saxophone
la trompette
le clavier
les percussions (f)
un instrument de
musique
un genre
tous les styles

Les gens et les animaux
les ado(lescent)s
la femme
le chef
le journaliste
le meilleur copain
la chorale
le chien
le village

Mission accomplie?

I can...

- Talk about playing musical instruments
- Give and justify opinions about music
- Describe clothes using a range of adjectives and colours
- Use the verbs *mettre* and *pouvoir*
- Describe objects and positions
- Describe a general impression

- Use familiar words and structures in new contexts
- Use possessive adjectives accurately
- Talk about things I have done using the perfect tense
- Describe a visit to somewhere I have been
- Talk about events in the past using *être* and *avoir* to form the perfect tense
- Accept and turn down invitations

Hugo
Qu'est-ce qu'on voit?

 Emma
On voit un musicien. Il joue du saxophone. On voit sa tête, ses cheveux et son nez.

 Hugo
Il a un gros nez!

 Emma
On voit aussi ses jambes et ses pieds…

 Lucas
C'est vrai, mais on voit aussi la tête d'une fille…

 Emma
La tête d'une fille? Où?

 Hugo
Regarde à droite. On voit les yeux, le nez, la bouche.

 Emma
Ah oui! À gauche, on voit un musicien et à droite on voit la tête d'une fille. Super!

 a Regarde l'image et lis les commentaires.
Look at the picture and read the comments.

b Trouve dans le texte l'équivalent français de:
Find in the text the French equivalent of:

1 What do we see?   2 We see a musician.

3 He's playing the saxophone.   4 his head, his hair, his nose

5 his legs and his feet   6 a girl's head

7 Look on the right.   8 her eyes, her nose, her mouth

9 on the left

2 À deux, regardez l'image et parlez.
In pairs, point at different parts of the picture and talk about what you see.

Exemple
On voit deux filles…

Jeunes filles au piano par Pierre-Auguste Renoir

3 Regarde le tableau et complète la description.
Look at the painting and complete the description.

bleue	colorée	mains	musique
piano	rouge	verte	voit

C'est un tableau de Pierre-Auguste Renoir. Au milieu, on **1** _____ une fille qui joue du **2** _____. C'est une scène très **3** _____: la pianiste porte une robe **4** _____ et sa sœur porte une robe **5** _____. On voit les bras et les **6** _____ de la pianiste et on pense qu'on va entendre la **7** _____.

4 Écoute. Quels commentaires sont positifs? Quels commentaires sont négatifs?
Listen. Which comments are positive and which are negative?

Exemple
1 positif

5 À deux. A décrit le tableau. B dit si c'est vrai ou faux. Ensuite, changez de rôles.
In pairs. A makes a comment about the painting. B says whether it's true or false. Then swap parts.

Exemple
A La pianiste porte une robe verte.
B C'est faux!

1 Tu me casses
les oreilles!

2 Elle danse
comme
un pied.

3 Ce gâteau me donne
l'eau à la bouche.

4 Elle fait
la tête!

5 Tu veux un
coup de main?

6 Mon petit frère est
casse-pieds!

1 **Pour chaque partie du corps, trouve une phrase avec le mot français équivalent.**
For each body part, find a sentence above that includes the equivalent French word.

a ears   **b** feet   **c** foot   **d** hand   **e** head   **f** mouth

2 **Choisis la bonne explication.**
Choose the right explanation.

1 Tu me casses les oreilles!

   a C'est trop bruyant.   **b** J'aime ta musique.

2 Elle danse comme un pied.

   a Elle danse très bien.   **b** Elle danse mal.

3 Ce gâteau me donne l'eau à la bouche.

   a Je voudrais manger ce gâteau.   **b** J'ai soif!

4 Elle fait la tête!

   a Elle n'est pas contente.   **b** Elle est très intelligente.

5 Tu veux un coup de main?

   a Tu n'es pas sympa.   **b** Je peux t'aider?

6 Mon petit frère est casse-pieds!

   a Mon petit frère est à l'hôpital.   **b** Mon petit frère est énervant.

3 **À deux. A mime une expression. B dit l'expression. Ensuite changez de rôles.**
In pairs. A mimes an expression. B chooses the right expression. Then swap roles.

Exemple   **A** *pretends to sulk.*
                B Tu fais la tête!

1

Il a perdu la tête!

2

Elle a couru à toutes jambes.

3

J'ai fait des pieds et des mains pour avoir une guitare.

4

Son violon a coûté les yeux de la tête!

5

Il est tombé nez à nez avec un lion.

a Traduis les phrases 1–5 en anglais 'mot à mot'.
Translate the sentences 1–5 into English 'word for word'.

b Trouve un idiome anglais équivalent pour chaque phrase.
Find an equivalent English saying for each sentence. There are lots of alternative answers.

Choisis la bonne explication.
Choose the right explanation.

1 Il a perdu la tête!

   a Il a perdu le match.   **b** Il est complètement bizarre.

2 Elle a couru à toutes jambes.

   a Elle est venue très rapidement.   **b** Elle n'est pas venue rapidement.

3 J'ai fait des pieds et des mains pour avoir une guitare.

   a J'ai fait beaucoup d'efforts pour avoir une guitare.   **b** Je joue très bien de la guitare.

4 Son violon a coûté les yeux de la tête!

   a Son violon est vraiment horrible.   **b** Son violon est très, très cher!

5 Il est tombé nez à nez avec un lion.

   a Il a rencontré un lion.   **b** Il a mangé un lion.

Écoute les phrases. Trouve le sujet de chaque phrase dans la liste.
Listen to sentences. For each sentence, choose who is being spoken about from the list.

je	tu	elle	mon piano	elles

Traduis ces phrases en français.
Use phrases from this page to translate the sentences into French.

a Are you sulking?   **b** Her coat cost a lot.   **c** Does he want a hand?

d She ran into her father.   **e** Your music is too loud!   **f** My parents are annoying.

g I play the piano very badly.   **h** They ran as fast as they could.

Le parc est sauvé!

Can you guess what will happen in the final episode of the bande dessinée? Read it and find out if you are right!

Résumé

Au poste de police, Lucas raconte l'histoire. Il a vu les plans de M. Vilain et M. Dupont. Ils veulent transformer le parc en parking et ils ont un plan pour mettre Mme Héros en prison. M. Vilain et M. Dupont sont attrapés. Le parc est sauvé et les hommes se disputent derrière les barreaux.

Il y a un article sur les amis dans le journal. Ils ont rencontré Mme Héros et ils sont célèbres! Ils ont des billets gratuits pour le festival de musique.

Au festival, ils s'amusent bien et ils regardent des groupes fantastiques. Lucie arrive et elle demande à Abdou s'il veut aller au cinéma. Il dit «oui», bien sûr!

Les amis sont d'accord: c'est génial d'avoir sauvé le parc et c'est super-génial d'avoir des billets gratuits pour le festival!

Activité

What happens next? Write your own episode of the bande dessinée *to continue the story.*

Reading skills

You have nearly reached the end of this book, and must have learned a good amount of vocabulary and grammatical structures. Now you can have fun reading all kinds of things in French. You don't need to know every single word to understand a text in a foreign language.

One of the first things to do is to get the main idea.
- Is there a heading or a title to help you?
- Is there a photo or an image that sets the scene?
- Can you spot helpful cognates (words that are spelled the same in French and in English) or near-cognates – like *art*, *sport*, *musique*, *parc*, or *culturel*?

Le Parc de La Villette

Le Parc de La Villette, situé dans l'est de Paris, est un énorme parc culturel. On y trouve des salles de concert, ainsi que la Cité de la musique et le Conservatoire national de musique et de danse.

Lis ce texte. Ça parle de quoi?
Read this text. What is it about?

a a park dedicated to the cinema   **b** a park dedicated to painting

c a park dedicated to music

When you come across an unfamiliar word, try to guess what kind of word it might be. Is it a verb (doing word), a noun (thing), an adjective (describing word) or something else? This technique will help you work out the word's meaning.

Pour chaque image, lis la phrase, puis fais le quiz.
For each picture, read the sentence, then do the quiz.

Beaucoup d'artistes peignent leur famille et leur maison.

1 The word *peignent* is most probably:

   a an adjective **b** a noun   **c** a verb

2 The word *peignent* most probably means:

   a hurt   **b** paint   **c** draw

3 Translate that sentence into English. Did you work out what the word *leur* means?

> Auguste Rodin est le nom d'un sculpteur.

4 The word *sculpteur* has most probably something to do with:

  a music   **b** painting   **c** sculpture

5 In French, many words ending in *–eur* (like *docteur, professeur, danseur*) are names of:

  a objects   **b** art forms   **c** occupations

6 The word *sculpteur* most probably means:

  a sculpture   **b** sculpting   **c** sculptor

7 Translate the sentence into English.

> Mon professeur de musique organise souvent des concerts merveilleux.

8 The word *merveilleux* is probably:

  a a verb   **b** a noun   **c** an adjective

9 The English equivalents of French words ending in *–eux* usually end in:

  a –ous   **b** –ing   **c** –ic

10 *Merveilleux* most probably means:

  a dramatic   **b** marvellous   **c** thrilling

11 Translate the sentence into English. Remember to think about the word order, which might not be the same in English as it is in French.

> You can also look for other clues so you know the general purpose of a sentence. Is it a question or a statement? Does it refer to the present, the past or the future?

Lis les phrases.
Read the sentences. Which sentences:

a refer to 'me'   **b** talk about the past   **c** talk about the future   **d** talk about the present?

1 Maeva joue du piano.

2 Je vais voir la Joconde.

3 Je vais aller au Centre Pompidou.

4 Je suis allée au musée du Louvre.

5 Tu vas monter à la tour Eiffel?

6 Abdou a écouté de la musique géniale.

7 Lucas regarde des tableaux de Picasso.

8 Sophie a visité le musée d'Orsay.

Pronunciation reference

Accented letters

Accents provide helpful information on pronunciation and help you tell apart different words with the same spellings. Here are two important accented letters:

ç	The cedilla mark under the letter 'c' (ç) before 'a', 'o' and 'u' makes it sound like the letter 's'. The letter 'c' always sounds like an 's' in front of 'e' and 'i'.	p8
é	A letter 'e' with an acute accent (é) is a more closed kind of 'e' (as in your tongue is closer to the roof of your mouth), more like 'may' than 'met': été	p8

Letter combinations

Some letter combinations sound very different in French compared to English. Here are some examples you will meet in this book:

aille	The letter combination *aille* is pronounced like the English word 'eye': *de taille moyenne*	p12
able	Words ending in –*able* are pronounced differently in French: *un portable*	p34
oi	In French, the letters 'oi' are pronounced 'wa': *moi*	p36
th	Remember that 'th' always sounds like the letter 't': *un thé à la menthe*	p90
au eau	When you combine an 'a' (or 'ea') with an 'u', it sounds like an 'o': *au Canada de l'eau*	p100
ou	The letters 'ou' are pronounced like the vowel sound in the English word 'soup': *nous vous beaucoup*	p100
ai ei	The combinations 'ai' and 'ei' are pronounced the: *Il fait du soleil.*	p100
eu	Also listen out for the sound of the letters 'eu': *il pleut deux*	p100

Silent endings and liaisons

Just like in English, some letters in French are silent. Here are some rules to help you remember which they are:

1	If a word ends in a 't', 's', 'd' or 'x', you don't pronounce the last letter: *intelligent, gros, bavard, cheveux*	p10
2	However, if a word ends in 'te', 'se' or 'de' you **do** pronounce the consonant: *intelligente, grosse, bavarde*	p10

3	If a word ending in 's' or 'x' is followed by a word beginning with a vowel, you pronounce the 's' or 'x' at the beginning of the next word. This is a **liaison**. *trois ans, deux ans, les amis*	p14
4	The *–ent* ending of verb corresponding to 'they' is not pronounced. *ils aim**ent***	p82

Phonics

You often don't get all of the information you need to pronounce a word from its spelling, so linguists use symbols from the International Phonetic Alphabet (IPA) to represent sounds. Here are all of the sounds used in French.

	Name	IPA symbol	Common spellings	Examples
Vowels	closed a	ɑ	as, â	**pas**, **pâte**
	open a	a	a	**ami**
	closed e	e	ai, é, es, er, ez, ei	j'**ai**, **été**, **les**, all**er**, ch**ez**, ens**ei**gner
	open e	ɛ	è, ê, e, ei, ai	m**è**re, t**ê**te, **est**, tr**ei**ze, f**ai**te
	mute e	ə	e	l**e**
	i	i	i, y	**i**l **y** a
	closed o	o	o, ô, au, eau	r**o**se, h**ô**tel, **au** Canada, l'**eau**
	open o	ɔ	o	p**o**mme
	closed eu	ø	eu, œu	il pl**eu**t, **œu**fs
	open eu	œ	eu, œu	profess**eu**r, s**œu**r
	ou	u	ou	n**ou**s
	u	y	u, û	t**u**, s**û**r
Nasal sounds	nasal a	ɑ̃	an, am, en, em	s**an**s, ch**am**bre, **en**fant, t**em**ps
	nasal e	ɛ̃	in, im	p**ain**, **im**patient
	nasal o	ɔ̃	on, om	s**on**, n**om**
	nasal eu	œ̃	un, um	**un**, parf**um**
Semi-vowels		j	l, i, ll, y	oe**il**, ad**i**eu, fi**ll**e, **y**eux
		w	oi, ou	m**oi**, **ou**i
		ɥ	u	n**u**it
Consonants		b	b	**b**on
		d	d	**d**ans
		f	f, ph	neu**f**, **ph**armacie
		g	g	**g**are
		k	c, ch, k, qu	sa**c**, **ch**aos, s**k**i, **qu**inze
		l	l, ll	**l**e, mi**ll**e
		m	m, mm	**m**agasin, fe**mm**e
		n	n, nn	**n**ez, bo**nn**e
		ɲ	gn	a**gn**eau
		p	p	**p**lage
		ʁ	r	**r**oue
		s	c, ç, s, ss, sc, ti	**c**inq, **ç**a, sa**c**, poi**ss**on, pi**sc**ine atten**ti**on
		ʃ	ch, sh	**ch**at, **sh**ort
		t	t, th	**t**out, **th**é
		v	v	**v**ous
		z	s, z	mai**s**on, **z**oo
		ʒ	g, j	**g**énial, **j**e

Verb tables

The majority of French verbs follow a regular pattern when you use them to form other tenses. There are two regular patterns: one for verbs ending in –er and one for verbs ending in –ir. You can learn more about regular verbs on page 130.

There are some verbs, called 'irregular verbs' which do not follow the usual patterns. Instead, they have their own patterns, which you should memorise. Here are the irregular verbs you will meet in this book.

aller (to go)
PRESENT

je	vais
tu	vas
il/elle/on	va
nous	allons
vous	allez
ils/elles	vont

PERFECT

je	suis allé(e)
tu	es allé(e)
il/elle/on	est allé(e)
nous	sommes allé(e)s
vous	êtes allé(e)(s)
ils/elles	sont allé(e)s

IMPERATIVE   va / allez

avoir (to have)
PRESENT

j'	ai
tu	as
il/elle/on	a
nous	avons
vous	avez
ils/elles	ont

PERFECT

j'	ai eu
tu	as eu
il/elle/on	a eu
nous	avons eu
vous	avez eu
ils/elles	ont eu

IMPERATIVE   aie / ayez

boire (to drink)
PRESENT

je	bois
tu	bois
il/elle/on	boit
nous	buvons
vous	buvez
ils/elles	boivent

PERFECT

j'	ai bu
tu	as bu
il/elle/on	a bu
nous	avons bu
vous	avez bu
ils/elles	ont bu

IMPERATIVE   bois / buvez

devoir (to have to)
PRESENT

je	dois
tu	dois
il/elle/on	doit
nous	devons
vous	devez
ils/elles	doivent

PERFECT

j'	ai dû
tu	as dû
il/elle/on	a dû
nous	avons dû
vous	avez dû
ils/elles	ont dû

IMPERATIVE   dois / devez

être (to be)
PRESENT

je	suis
tu	es
il/elle/on	est
nous	sommes
vous	êtes
ils/elles	sont

PERFECT

j'	ai été
tu	as été
il/elle/on	a été
nous	avons été
vous	avez été
ils/elles	ont été

IMPERATIVE   sois / soyez

faire (to do; to make)

PRESENT

je	fais
tu	fais
il/elle/on	fait
nous	faisons
vous	faites
ils/elles	font

PERFECT

j'	ai fait
tu	as fait
il/elle/on	a fait
nous	avons fait
vous	avez fait
ils/elles	ont fait

IMPERATIVE   fais / faites

mettre (to put)

PRESENT

je	mets
tu	mets
il/elle/on	met
nous	mettons
vous	mettez
ils/elles	mettent

PERFECT

j'	ai mis
tu	as mis
il/elle/on	a mis
nous	avons mis
vous	avez mis
ils/elles	ont mis

IMPERATIVE   mets / mettez

pouvoir (to be able)

PRESENT

je	peux
tu	peux
il/elle/on	peut
nous	pouvons
vous	pouvez
ils/elles	peuvent

PERFECT

j'	ai pu
tu	as pu
il/elle/on	a pu
nous	avons pu
vous	avez pu
ils/elles	ont pu

IMPERATIVE   *not used*

prendre (to take)

PRESENT

je	prends
tu	prends
il/elle/on	prend
nous	prenons
vous	prenez
ils/elles	prennent

PERFECT

j'	ai pris
tu	as pris
il/elle/on	a pris
nous	avons pris
vous	avez pris
ils/elles	ont pris

IMPERATIVE   prends / prenez

voir (to see)

PRESENT

je	vois
tu	vois
il/elle/on	voit
nous	voyons
vous	voyez
ils/elles	voient

PERFECT

j'	ai vu
tu	as vu
il/elle/on	a vu
nous	avons vu
vous	avez vu
ils/elles	ont vu

IMPERATIVE   vois / voyez

vouloir (to want)

PRESENT

je	veux
tu	veux
il/elle/on	veut
nous	voulons
vous	voulez
ils/elles	veulent

PERFECT

j'	ai voulu
tu	as voulu
il/elle/on	a voulu
nous	avons voulu
vous	avez voulu
ils/elles	ont voulu

IMPERATIVE   veuille / veuillez

The present tense

Using regular –er verbs

In French, the most common type of verbs are –er verbs, like *habiter* (to live). This is how they work:

*j'habit**e***	I live
*tu habit**es***	you live
il/elle/on habite	he/she/we live(s)
nous habit**ons**	we live
vouz habit**ez**	you live
il/elles habit**ent**	they live

Irregular verbs

There are some verbs, called 'irregular verbs', which do not follow the usual patterns. Instead, they have their own patterns, which you should memorise. The verbs *être* (to be) and *avoir* (to have) are both irregular. To see how they work, look at pages 128–129.

Making a negative sentence

Use *ne* and *pas* around a verb to make it negative. For example:
*Je **ne** suis **pas** timide.*   I'm not shy.

Use *ne* and *jamais* around a verb to mean 'never'. For example:
*Je **ne** rate **jamais** le bus.*   I never miss the bus.

Using reflexive verbs

A reflexive verb is just the same as any other verb, but it also has a small word called a reflexive pronoun, which comes before it.

*je **me** lève*	I get up
*tu **te** lèves*	you get up
*il/elle **se** lève*	he/she gets up
*on **se** lève*	we get up

Pronouns

Tu and *vous*

There are two French words for 'you'.
- Use *tu* to talk to one person you know well.
- Use *vous* to talk to more than one person, or to someone you don't know very well.

Ils and *elles*

There are also two French words for 'they'.
Use *ils* to talk about
- a group of people that includes at least one male
- masculine plural nouns (or a group of masculine and feminine nouns).

Use *elles* to talk about
- a group of women
- feminine plural nouns.

Using *on* to mean 'we'

On is an informal way of saying 'we'. Use the same form of verb as for 'he' or 'she'.

Using nouns

All French nouns are either masculine or feminine, not just nouns to do with people. Use *le* (the) or *un* (a/an) with a masculine noun and *la* (the) or *une* (a/an) with a feminine noun:

le marché   the market   *la ville*   the town/city   *un cinéma*   a cinema
une église   a church

To talk about more than one item, use *les* or *des*:
les magasins   the shops   *des magasins*   some shops

Possessives

There are three French words for 'my', 'your' and 'his/her'. To know which word to use, check whether the noun that comes after it is masculine, feminine or plural. Note that there is no difference in French between 'his' and 'her'.

	masculine	feminine	plural
my	*mon*	*ma*	*mes*
your	*ton*	*ta*	*tes*
his/her	*son*	*sa*	*ses*

How to say 'some'

Use *du* for masculine nouns: *du jambon*
Use *de la* for feminine nouns: *de la limonade*
Use *des* for plural nouns: *des pommes*
Use *de l'* for nouns beginning with a vowel or silent 'h': *de l'eau*

Making a noun plural

In most cases, add 's' just like in English: *J'ai deux frères.*   I have two brothers.

Talking about what belongs to someone

Use *de* (or *d'* before a vowel):
le frère de Marie   Marie's brother   *la guitare d'Abdou*   Abdou's guitar

Using prepositions

Use prepositions to talk about where things are:
Ma guitare est sous le lit.   My guitar is under the bed.

Using adjectives

French adjectives change depending on the noun they describe. Most go after the noun. Usually, you add an 'e' for feminine nouns and an 's' for plural nouns:

*un tee-shirt **bleu***   a blue tee-shirt
*des tee-shirts **bleus***   blue tee-shirts
*une chaussure **bleue***   a blue shoe
*des chaussures **bleues***   blue shoes

When the adjective already ends in 'e', there is no need to add a second.
Some adjectives are irregular.

	ms	mpl	fs	fpl
beautiful	beau	beaux	belle	belles
white	blanc	blancs	blanche	blanches
brown	marron	marron	marron	marron

Places and directions

Cities, countries and continents

When used with the name of a city, the word à can mean 'in' or 'to':

Je suis à Paris.	I am in Paris.
Je vais à Marseille.	I am going to Marseille.

Use *en* with feminine countries and continents and *au* with masculine:

Il va aller au Sénégal, en Afrique.   He is going to go to Senegal, in Africa.

Saying 'to the'

Use *au* for masculine places: *au cinéma*
Use *à la* for feminine places: *à la plage*
Use *aux* for places which are plural: *aux marionnettes*
Use *à l'* if the place begins with a vowel or silent 'h': *à l'exposition*

Asking questions

Use *quel* with masculine words and *quelle* with feminine words to mean 'which' or 'what':

C'est quel genre de parc?   What kind of park is it?

Quand means 'when' and *où* means 'where':

Tu vas aller où?	Where are you going to go?
Tu vas y aller quand?	When are you going to go?

Dates and time

Telling the time

To ask the time, say *Quelle heure est-il?* To tell the time, use the phrase *Il est*.

Il est cinq heures.	It's five o'clock.
Il est deux heures dix.	It's ten past two.
Il est huit heures moins cinq.	It's five to eight.
Il est cinq heures et quart.	It's quarter past five.
Il est une heure moins le quart.	It's quarter to one.
Il est deux heures et demie.	It's half past two.

The 24-hour clock is very often used in France:

Il est quinze heures.   It's 3 p.m.

To use the 12-hour clock in French, use the phrases *du matin* and *du soir*:

Il est huit heures du matin.	It's 8 a.m.
Il est neuf heures du soir.	It's 9 p.m.

Use the preposition à to say what time you do something:

Je me lève à huit heures.   I get up at eight o'clock.

Birthdays

To say your birthday month, use 'en' before the month. To say your birthday date, use 'le' before the date:

Mon anniversaire est en mai.	My birthday is in May.
Mon anniversaire est le 15 mai.	My birthday is on 15 May.

Sports and activities

To talk about what sports and activities you do:
Use *faire du* or *jouer au* for masculine activities: *Je joue du piano.*
Use *faire de la* or *jouer à la* for feminine activities: *Je fais de la danse.*
Use *faire de l'* or *jouer à l'* if the activity begins with a vowel: *Je fais de l'escrime.*

The weather

To ask what the weather is like, say: *Quel temps fait-il?* You can answer like this:

Il pleut.	It's raining.
Il fait beau.	The weather is nice.
Il y a du soleil.	It's sunny.

Making suggestions

Pouvoir means 'to be able to'. *Vouloir* means 'to want'.

je peux	I can	*je veux*	I want
tu peux	you can	*tu veux*	you want
il/elle/on peut	he/she/we can	*il/elle/on veut*	he/she/we want(s)

You can follow either of these verbs with a verb in its infinitive form:
Au parc on peut jouer au tennis.   You can play tennis in the park.

Je voudrais means 'I would like' and *on pourrait* means 'we could':

Je voudrais aller à Dakar.	I'd like to go to Dakar.
On pourrait regarder la compétition.	We could watch the competition.

Using the imperative

To give instructions or advice, use the imperative:

	Informal (people you say *tu* to)	Formal (people you say *vous* to)
Listen!	*Écoute!*	*Écoutez!*
Be careful!	*Fais attention!*	*Faites attention!*

Using *aller* to talk about the future

Use *aller* in the present tense and a verb in the infinitive to say what is going to happen:
Je vais aller au Maroc.   I'm going to go to Morocco.

The perfect tense

The perfect tense with *avoir*

To make the perfect tense, you use the present tense of *avoir* followed by a form of the verb called the past participle. To make the past participle of –er verbs, remove the –er ending and replace it with é. Once you know the past participle, you can follow the same rule with *tu, il, elle* and *on*:

j'ai aimé	I liked
tu as aimé	you liked
il/elle/on a aimé	he/she/we liked

Place *ne ... pas* around the *avoir* part to make a negative:
*je **n**'ai **pas** aimé*   I didn't like

Some past participles are irregular:

j'ai fait	I did	*j'ai vu*	I saw

The perfect tense with *être*

Some common verbs use the present tense of *être* instead of *avoir* to make the perfect tense. The past participle is formed in the same way but you need to add an extra e at the end of the past participle if the action is performed by a female:

aller	*rester*
je suis allé(e)	*je suis resté(e)*
tu es allé(e)	*tu es resté(e)*
il est allé	*il est resté*
elle est allée	*elle est restée*
on est allé(e)(s)	*on est resté(e)(s)*

Aa

à bientôt	excl	see you soon
à motifs	adj	patterned
à tour de rôle	adv	in turn
admirer	vb	to admire
ado(lescent)	nm	teenager
adorer	vb	to love
affaires	npl	belongings
Afrique	nf	Africa
âge	nm	age
ah bon?	excl	oh really?
aimer	vb	to like
album photos	nm	photo album
aller au lit	vb	to go to bed
Amérique du nord	nf	North America
Amérique du sud	nf	South America
ami(e)	nm/f	friend
amour	nm	love
anglais	nm	English (language)
anglais(e)	adj	English
Angleterre	nf	England
année	nf	year
anniv(ersaire)	nm	birthday
Antarctique	nm	Antarctica
août	nm	August
appartement	nm	flat, appartment
appeler	vb	to call
apprendre	vb	to learn
après	prep	after

après-midi	nm	afternoon
aquarium	nm	fish tank
arabe	nm	Arabic (language)
armoire	nf	wardrobe
arroser	vb	to water
art	nm	art
arts plastiques	npl	art
ascenseur	nm	lift, elevator
Asie	nf	Asia
assez	adv	quite
athlétisme	nm	athletics
attraper	vb	to catch
au milieu	adv	in the middle
au secours!	excl	help!
aujourd'hui	adv	today
aussi	adv	also
Australie	nf	Australia
automne	nm	autumn
autre	adj	other
avec	prep	with
avis	nm	opinion
avoir faim	vb	to be hungry
avoir peur	vb	to be scared
avoir soif	vb	to be thirsty
avril	nm	April

Bb

balade	nf	walk, stroll
ballon	nm	ball
ballon de basket	nm	basketball (item)

barbecue	nm	barbecue
barreaux	npl	bars (on window)
basket	nm	basketball (sport)
bâtiment	nm	building
bavard(e)	adj	chatty
beau (f belle)	adj	beautiful
beaucoup	adv	a lot
belge	adj	Belgian
beurre	nm	butter
bibliothèque	nf	library
bien	adv	well
bien!	excl	right!
bien sûr	excl	of course
blanc (f blanche)	adj	white
bleu(e)	adj	blue
blond(e)	adj	blond
blues	nm	blues (music)
bof!	excl	something to say if you're not bothered
boire	vb	to drink
bonjour	excl	hello, good morning
bord de la mer	nm	seaside
botte	nf	boot
bouche	nf	mouth
boulot	nm	job (informal)
boxe	nf	boxing
bras	nm	arm
britannique	adj	British
brun(e)	adj	brown
bruyant(e)	adj	noisy

Cc

campagne	nf	countryside
Canada	nm	Canada
canadien(ne)	adj	Canadian
carte	nf	card, map, menu
cartes	npl	cards
casser	vb	to break
ce(tte)	adj	this
centre commercial	nm	shopping centre
centre d'équitation	nm	riding centre
chacun(e)	pron	each
chaise	nf	chair
chambre	nf	bedroom
champignon	nm	mushroom
chanter	vb	to sing
chapeau	nm	hat
chaque	adj	every, each
chaud(e)	adj	warm, hot
chaussette	nf	sock
chef	nm	chief
chemise	nf	shirt
cher (f chère)	adj	expensive
cheveux	npl	hair
chez moi	adv	at my house
chien	nm	dog
chocolat	nm	chocolate
chocolat chaud	nm	hot chocolate
choisir	vb	to choose
chorale	nf	choir

ciel	nm	sky
cinéma	nm	cinema
circulation	nf	circulation
classique	adj	classical
clavier	nm	keyboard
clé	nf	key
climatisation	nf	air conditioning
cola	nm	cola
coloré(e)	adj	colourful
commander	vb	to order
comme ci, comme ça	adv	so-so
comme d'habitude	adv	as usual
commencer	vb	to start
comment	adv	how, what
compétition	nf	competition
comprendre	vb	to understand
concert	nm	concert
copain (f copine)	nm/f	friend
correspondant(e)	nm/f	penpal
cours	nm	class (lessons)
courses	npl	shopping
court(e)	adj	short
créole	nm	Creole (language)
crêpe	nf	sweet pancake
crêperie	nf	creperie, pancake house
Croix-Rouge	nf	Red Cross
cuisine	nf	kitchen

Dd

d'abord	adv	first
d'accord!	excl	okay
dans	prep	in
danse	nf	dance
danser	vb	to dance
de taille moyenne	adj	of average height
de temps en temps	adv	occasionally
de toutes les couleurs	adj	multicoloured
décembre	nm	December
déjà	adv	already
dernier (f dernière)	adj	last
dernier étage	nm	top floor
derrière	adv	behind
détester	vb	to hate
devant	adv	in front
devoirs	npl	homework
différence	nf	difference
difficile	adj	difficult
dimanche	nm	Sunday
dîner	vb	to have dinner
dinosaure	nm	dinosaur
donc	conj	so
droite	adj	right (not left)
drôle	adj	funny

Ee

eau	nf	water
écouter	vb	to listen

écrire	vb	to write
église	nf	church
électrique	adj	electric
en fait	adv	in fact
enfant	nm	child
ennuyeux (f ennuyeuse)	adj	boring
ensuite	adv	then, next
entre	prep	between
environ	adv	about
EPS	nf	PE
équitation	nf	horse riding
escrime	nf	fencing
est	nm	east
et	conj	and
étagère	nf	shelf
été	nm	summer
Europe	nf	Europe
exister	vb	to exist
exposition	nf	exhibition

Ff

facile	adj	easy
faim	nf	hunger
faire du ski	vb	to ski?
faire du vélo	vb	to cycle?
famille	nf	family
fatigué(e)	adj	tired
faux	adj	false, wrong
femme	nf	woman, wife
ferme	nf	farm

fête	nf	party
février	nm	February
film	nm	film
fils unique (f fille unique)	nm/f	only child
finalement	adv	finally
fleuve	nm	river
flûte	nf	flute
fois	nf	time (occasion)
fontaine	nf	fountain
français	nm	French (language)
français(e)	adj	French
France	nf	France
frère	nm	brother
froid(e)	adj	cold
fromage	nm	cheese
futsal	nm	futsal (indoor five-a-side football)

Gg

galette	nf	savoury pancake
gare	nf	station
gâteau	nm	cake
gauche	adj	left (not right)
génial(e)	adj	brilliant
genre	nm	style, type
gens	npl	people
géographie	nf	geography
grand(e)	adj	tall, big
gratuit(e)	adj	free

gris(e)	adj	grey
gros(se)	adj	big, fat
guitare	nf	guitar
gymnastique	nf	gymnastics

Hh

habiter	vb	to live
handball	nm	handball
harpe	nf	harp
herbe	nf	grass
hip hop	nm	hip-hop
histoire	nf	story, history
hiver	nm	winter

Ii

ici	adv	here
image	nf	picture
impatient(e)	adj	impatient
impressionnant(e)	adj	impressive
informatique	nf	ICT
instrument de musique	nm	musical instrument
intelligent(e)	adj	intelligent
intéressant(e)	adj	interesting
italien(ne)	adj	Italian

Jj

jambe	nf	leg
jambon	nm	ham
janvier	nm	January

jardin	nm	garden
jaune	adj	yellow
jean	nm	jeans
jeu	nm	game
jeudi	nm	Thursday
jeune	adj	young
Jeux olympiques	npl	Olympic Games
jouer	vb	to play
journaliste	nm/f	journalist
juillet	nm	July
juin	nm	June
jupe	nf	skirt
jus de fruit	nm	fruit juice
juste à temps	adv	just in time

Ll

langue officielle	nf	official language
limonade	nm	lemonade
lire	vb	to read
lit	nm	bed
littérature	nf	literature
long(ue)	adj	long
louer	vb	to rent
lundi	nm	Monday

Mm

magasin	nm	shop
mai	nm	May
maillot de bain	nm	swimsuit

main	nf	hand
mais	conj	but
maison	nf	house
mal	adv	badly
malade	adj	ill
maman	nf	mum
manger	vb	to eat
manteau	nm	winter coat
marché	nm	market
mardi	nm	Tuesday
marionnettes	npl	a puppet show
marocain(e)	adj	Moroccan
marron	adj	brown
mars	nm	March
martiniquais(e)	adj	from Martinique
Martinique	nf	Martinique
maths	npl	maths
matière	nf	subject
matin	nm	morning
meilleur copain	nm	best friend
menu à 12,50€	nm	12.50€ menu
mer	nf	sea
merci	excl	thank you, thanks
mercredi	nm	Wednesday
mère	nf	mother
métal	nm	metal (music)
mettre	vb	to put on, wear
mi-long(ue)	adj	medium-length
mince	adj	thin
moche	adj	ugly

mode	nf	fashion
moderne	adj	modern
moi	pron	me
moins	adv	less
moins	prep	to (when telling the time)
mois	nm	month
monde	nm	world
monstre	nm	monster
montagne	nf	mountain
montagnes russes	npl	rollercoasters
montre	nf	watch
musée	nm	museum
musique	nf	music

Nn

nager	vb	to swim
natation	nf	swimming
neige	nf	snow
neiger	vb	to snow
nettoyer	vb	to clean
nez	nm	nose
noir(e)	adj	black
nord	nm	north
normalement	adv	usually
nouilles	npl	noodles
Nouvelle-Calédonie	nf	New Caledonia
novembre	nm	November
nul	adj	rubbish

Oo

octobre	nm	October
œuf	nm	egg
oignon	nm	onion
oncle	nm	uncle
orange	adj	orange
ordinateur	nm	computer
oreille	nf	ear
où	adv	where
oublier	vb	to forget
ouest	nm	west

Pp

pain	nm	bread
pantalon	nm	trousers
papa	nm	dad
par an	prep	a year, per year
par contre	adv	on the other hand
par jour	prep	a day, per day
parc	nm	park
parce que	conj	because
parent	nm	parent
paresseux (f paresseuse)	adj	lazy
parler	vb	to speak
partager	vb	to share
partir	vb	to go, to leave
parvis	nm	square
pas	adv	not
pas d'accord	excl	I disagree

pas du tout	adv	not at all
passer	vb	to spend
passionnant(e)	adj	exciting
patinoire	nf	ice-rink
pays	nm	country
penser	vb	to think
percussions	npl	percussion
père	nm	father
personnage	nm	character
personne	nf	person
pétanque	nf	boules
petit(e)	adj	small, short
petit-déjeuner	nm	breakfast
un peu	nm	a little / a bit
un peu de tout	nm	a bit of everything
peur	nf	fear
piano	nm	piano
pied	nm	foot
piscine	nf	swimming pool
pizza	nf	pizza
place	nf	town square
plage	nf	beach
planche à voile	nf	windsurfing
plante	nf	plant
pleuvoir	vb	to rain
plongée	nf	diving
plongée sous-marine	nf	scuba diving
pluie	nf	rain
plus	adv	more

pomme	nf	apple
pont	nm	bridge
port	nm	port
portable	nm	mobile phone
porte	nf	door
portefeuille	nm	wallet
porter	vb	to wear
possible	adj	possible
poste de police	nm	police station
pouf-poire	nm	beanbag
pourquoi	adv	why
pouvoir	vb	to be able to
pratique	adj	practical
préféré(e)	adj	favourite
préférer	vb	to prefer
principal(e)	adj	main
printemps	nm	spring
proposer	vb	to offer
pull	nm	jumper

Qq

quand	conj, adv	when
quart	nm	quarter
quel dommage!	excl	what a pity!
quel(le)	adj	what, which
quelle horreur!	excl	how awful!
quelquefois	adv	sometimes
qui	pron	who
quitter	vb	to leave

Rr

R&B	nm	R&B
raconter une histoire	vb	to tell a story
raisonnable	adj	sensible
ranger	vb	to tidy
rarement	adv	rarely
rater	vb	to miss
regarder	vb	to watch
reggae	nm	reggae
région	nf	region
rentrer	vb	to go home
renverser	vb	to spill
rester	vb	to stay
robe	nf	dress
rock	nm	rock (music)
roller	nm	roller-blading
rose	adj	pink
rouge	adj	red
roux (f rousse)	adj	red (hair)
rue	nf	street
rugby	nm	rugby
ruines	npl	ruins

Ss

saison des pluies	nf	rainy season
saison sèche	nf	dry season
salade	nf	salad
salé(e)	adj	savoury
salle de bains	nf	bathroom
salle à manger	nf	dining room

salon	nm	living room
salut	excl	hi
samedi	nm	Saturday
sans	prep	without
sauver	vb	to save
saxophone	nm	saxophone
sciences	npl	sciences
se coucher	vb	to go to bed
se disputer	vb	to argue
se laver	vb	to have a wash
se lever	vb	to get up
séjour	nm	a stay
semaine	nf	week
Sénégal	nm	Senegal
sénégalais(e)	adj	Senegalese
septembre	nm	September
seulement	adv	only
s'habiller	vb	to get dressed
short	nm	shorts
skate	nm	skateboarding
skate-parc	nm	skatepark
sœur	nf	sister
soif	nf	thirst
soir	nm	evening
soirée	nf	evening
soirée pyjama	nf	pyjama party
sol	nm	floor
soleil	nm	sunshine
son et lumière	nm	sound and light (show)

sortie	nf	outing
sortir	vb	to go out
sous	prep	under, underneath
souvent	adv	often
spectacle	nm	show
stade	nm	stadium
stressé(e)	adj	stressed
style	nm	style
sucre	nm	sugar
sucré(e)	adj	sweet
sud	nm	south
super	adj	great, fantastic
sur	prep	over, on top
surtout	adv	especially
sweat(-shirt)	nm	sweatshirt
sympa	adj	friendly, nice

Tt

table	nf	table
tableau	nm	painting
tablette	nf	tablet
tajine	nm	tagine
tante	nf	aunt
tapis	nm	rug
technologie	nf	technology
temps	nm	time, weather
tennis	nm	tennis
tenue	nf	outfit
tête	nf	head

thé à menthe	nm	mint tea
théâtre	nm	drama
timide	adj	shy
tomate	nf	tomato
tomber	vb	to fall
toujours	adv	still, always
tous les jours	adv	every day
tout(e)	adj	all
tranquille	adj	quiet
très	adv	very
triste	adj	sad
trompette	nf	trumpet
trop	adv	too much
trottinette	nf	scooter
trouver	vb	to find, to think
Tunisie	nf	Tunisia
tunisien(ne)	adj	Tunisian

Vv

vaisselle	nf	washing up
vendredi	nm	Friday
vent	nm	wind
vers	prep	around (time)
vert(e)	adj	green
veste	nf	jacket

vêtement	nm	clothes
vietnamien(ne)	adj	Vietnamese
village	nm	village
ville	nf	town, city
violent(e)	adj	violent
violet(te)	adj	purple
violon	nm	violin
visite	nf	visit
voile	nf	sailing
voir	vb	to see
volcan	nm	volcano
vouloir	vb	to want
voyage	nm	journey
vrai(e)	adj	true
vraiment	adv	really
vue	nf	view

Ww

| week-end | nm | weekend |
| wolof | nm | Wolof (language) |

Yy

| yeux | npl | eyes |

Classroom instructions

Dans le livre...	In the book...
Écoute.	Listen.
Écoute encore.	Listen again.
Écris.	Write.
Lis.	Read.
Relis.	Reread.
Parle.	Speak.
Répète.	Repeat.
Complète les phrases.	Complete the sentences.
Corrige les phrases.	Correct the sentences.
Fais un sondage.	Do a survey.
Fais une liste.	Make a list.
Regarde les images.	Look at the pictures.
Remplis les blancs.	Fill the gaps.
Réponds à la question.	Answer the question.
Traduis en anglais.	Translate into English.
Traduis en français.	Translate into French.
Vérifie tes réponses.	Check your answers.
Vrai ou faux?	True or false?
Que...?	What...?
Qui...?	Who...?

En classe...	In class...
En groupes...	In groups...
À deux...	In pairs...
À trois...	In threes...
Prenez une feuille de papier.	Take out paper.
Ouvrez le livre.	Open the book.
Fermez le livre.	Close the book.
Asseyez-vous.	Sit down.
Levez-vous!	Stand up!
Silence!	Silence!
Rangez vos affaires!	Tidy up your things!
J'ai fini!	I've finished!
Je ne comprends pas!	I don't understand!
Voilà!	There you go!
Merci	Thank you
S'il vous plaît	Please
Oui Mademoiselle ...	Yes, Miss ...
Bonjour Madame ...	Hello Mrs ...
Au revoir Monsieur ...	Goodbye Mr ...